Polymer Clay
for the first time®

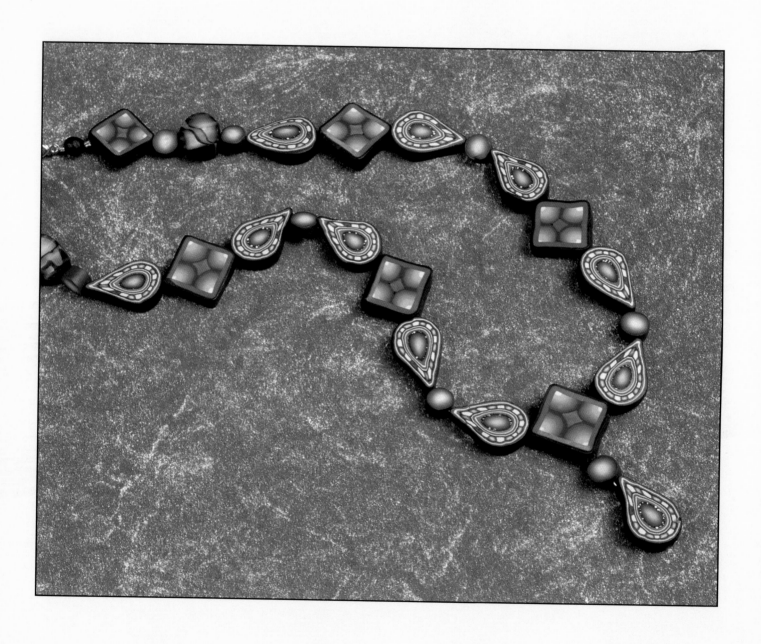

Polymer Clay
for the first time®

syndee holt

Sterling Publishing Co., Inc.
New York

Owner: Jo Packham

Editor: Leslie Ridenour

Staff: Marie Barber, Ann Bear, Areta Bingham, Kass Burchett,
Rebecca Christensen, Brenda Doncouse, Dana Durney,
Marilyn Goff, Holly Hollingsworth, Susan Jorgensen,
Barbara Milburn, Linda Orton, Karmen Quinney, Cindy Stoeckl,
Gina Swapp

Special Thanks

All projects in this book were created with outstanding and
innovative products provided by the following manufacturers
and retailers: the **Clay Factory** of Escondido, California
(www.clayfactoryinc.com) and **Polyform Products** of Elk Grove
Village, California, (www.sculpey.com) for clay products;
General Bead (www.genbead.com) for bracelet forms, jewelry
findings, and Tigertail; **Kemper** for cutters and tools; **Rupert,
Gibbon, and Spider** (Jacquard) for Pearl-X products; **Sanford**
for Prismacolor pencils; **Speedball** for brayers; and **Wild West
Distributors** for GellyRollers.

Library of Congress Cataloging-in-Publication Data

Holt, Syndee.
  Polymer clay for the first time / Syndee Holt.
    p.cm.

  Includes index.
  ISBN 0-8069-6827-3
   1.Polymer clay craft. I. Title.
  TT297 .H59 2000
  731.4`2—dc21   99-053579

10 9 8 7 6 5 4 3

Published in paperback in 2005 by Sterling Publishing Co., Inc.
387 Park Avenue South, New York, NY 10016
© 2000 by Chapelle Ltd.
Distributed in Canada by Sterling Publishing
℅ Canadian Manda Group, 165 Dufferin Street,
Toronto, Ontario, Canada M6K 3H6
Distributed in the United Kingdom by GMC Distribution services,
Castle Place, 166 High Street, Lewes, East Sussex, England BN7 1XU
Distributed in Australia by Capricorn Link (Australia) Pty Ltd.,
P.O. Box 704, Windsor, NSW 2756, Australia
Printed in China
All Rights Reserved
Sterling ISBN 0-8069-6827-3 Hardcover
         ISBN 1-4027-2705-4 Paperback

For information about custom editions, special sales, premium and
corporate purchases, please contact Sterling Special Sales
Department at 800-805-5489 or specialsales@sterlingpub.com.

Every effort has been made to
ensure that all of the information
in this book is accurate. However,
due to differing conditions, tools,
and individual skills, the publisher
cannot be responsible for any
injuries, losses, and/or any other
damages which may result from
the use of the information in this
book.

syndee holt can be reached at
the San Diego Polymer Clay Guild
website, at home via e-mail, or
through Polyform Products:

San Diego Polymer Clay Guild
website: www.myart.com/sdpcg
e-mail: syndeeh@gateway.net
Polyform Products: (847)427-0020

Other Helpful Clay Sources:
Krause's Arts and Crafts Magazine
Bead and Button Magazine
Jewelry Crafts Magazine
Crafts Magazine
www.delphi.com/polymerclay
www.npcg.org/home.html

About the Author

syndee holt is a middle-aged single mom who definitely doesn't fit that stereotype. She works full-time at UCSD as the Business Officer for Health Sciences Communications, who puts up with her disappearing to travel the country for the sake of polymer clay and always welcomes her back. She is the president of the San Diego Polymer Clay Guild and correspondence secretary of the National Polymer Clay Guild, as well as a member of the Spanish Village Artist Association in Balboa Park. She is an independent artist/designer for Polyform Products, performing in teaching, demonstrating, and writing capacities.

syndee's Fine Art degree is in photography. Hence, the photographs in the book were designed and executed by her and Kevin Walsh of UCSD Office of Learning Resources.

Her two sons, Tahichi and Koji, are busy becoming artists and writers themselves and are definitely part of her design team, along with the various lizards, cats, frogs, and stray children that make their home with them.

Dedication

This is for anyone who ever said, "I'd love to do that, but I don't have the time." If I can do it, so can you!

Acknowledgments

This small step in polymer and milestone in my life would not have been possible without the creative support of my sons, Tahichi and Koji, and my best buddy, my dad. Debu, your donations of home-cooked meals gave me more time to write without missing a beat.

Marie Segal is the embodiment of the words, "mentor," "friend," and "master artisan." I will always have space in my suitcase for your overflow. Howard, you are always there for polymer clayers and you give the best hugs!

Chuck Steinmann, you are "the bomb." Jan, Wayne, Hope, George, and the rest of the Polyform team—you're the greatest. You've given us some of the best arts and crafts products on the market, while making each individual clay crafter feel like they count. I am truly honored to be one of the Polyform Girls!

Thanks to Dr. Karen Garman at USCD OLR for your ecstatic support of this project as well as the use of your photo studios and personnel.

Terry B. Miller, your enthusiastic support for my work is matched only by your ability to drive me nuts. You have taught me patience and kept me smiling all the while.

syndee holt

Table
of Contents

**Polymer Clay
for the First Time**
8

**Section 1:
Polymer Clay Basics**
10

What do I need
to get started?
12

Section 2: Basic Canes
26

How do I make a pinroll cane?
Small Candleholder   28

How do I resize and reshape a pinroll cane?
Earrings   30

How do I recombine the pinroll cane?
Napkin Rings   32

How do I turn the pinroll cane inside out?
Mobius Bead   34

How do I make a bull's eye cane?
Clay Frame   38

How do I use the bull's eye cane?
Lacy Ornament   40

How do I add a banner to the bull's eye cane?
Buttons   42

How do I use the banner cane?
Twisted Beads   44

How do I make a feather cane?
Postage Stamp Collage   46

How do I make a checkerboard cane?
Covered Pen   48

How do I make a blended cane
using the Skinner method?
Light Switch Cover   51

How do I make 3-D chain-linked canes?
3-D Chain-linked Necklace   55

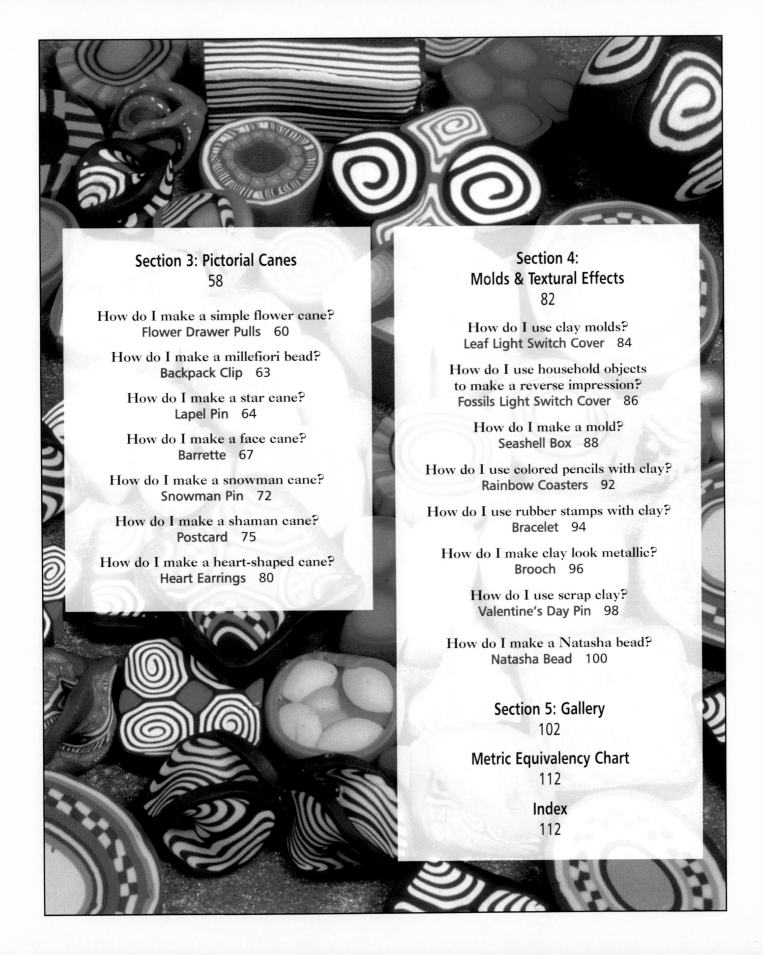

Section 3: Pictorial Canes
58

How do I make a simple flower cane?
Flower Drawer Pulls   60

How do I make a millefiori bead?
Backpack Clip   63

How do I make a star cane?
Lapel Pin   64

How do I make a face cane?
Barrette   67

How do I make a snowman cane?
Snowman Pin   72

How do I make a shaman cane?
Postcard   75

How do I make a heart-shaped cane?
Heart Earrings   80

Section 4:
Molds & Textural Effects
82

How do I use clay molds?
Leaf Light Switch Cover   84

How do I use household objects
to make a reverse impression?
Fossils Light Switch Cover   86

How do I make a mold?
Seashell Box   88

How do I use colored pencils with clay?
Rainbow Coasters   92

How do I use rubber stamps with clay?
Bracelet   94

How do I make clay look metallic?
Brooch   96

How do I use scrap clay?
Valentine's Day Pin   98

How do I make a Natasha bead?
Natasha Bead   100

Section 5: Gallery
102

Metric Equivalency Chart
112

Index
112

Polymer Clay for the first time

Introduction

My son once told me that every time you open a book, you are beginning a new path in your expanding universe. Well, by opening this book, you have certainly taken your first step. I get to be your tour-guide to the world of polymer clay. Polymer clay is more than just a space-age modeling material—it is a worldwide community of people dedicated to art, science, chemistry, and each other. It's one of the few art mediums where information between artists is shared freely, via the internet, videos, books, magazines, and guilds. I will introduce you to a few of my polymer clay artist friends throughout this book, they are artists, doctors, authors, teachers, and scientists—all drawn together by this medium and all very important in my life as friends and clay mentors.

Polymer clay is a plastic material first designed over thirty years ago for doll-making and molding. We've now expanded the techniques to include everything from cane-making (creating patterns in the clay), stamping, textures, faux stone, faux metals, transfers, and multimedia collage, to name a few. Artists are even turning the material on the lathe and throwing it on the potter's wheel. Because the baking temperature is so low, you can cover almost any other material with polymer clay to create new lamps, boxes, vases, frames, etc. It is waterproof, fade-proof, and durable.

I do need to warn you, though. Working with polymer clay is addictive. You'll live, breathe, and think clay 24 hours a day. You'll begin to see colors, textures, and ideas every-where. And you'll wake up at 2 a.m. with the idea to put them all together with your precious clay. AND once you do, you will be rushing to your computer, phone, or guild to share "the newest idea" with your other clay buddies. Personally, I couldn't ask for a better way to live!

Naturally, this means other things in life, like jobs, housework, cooking, children, family, and friends have to fight for our attention. But, don't overlook them—they are wonderful sources of ideas, support, and most important—tools!

How to Use This Book

Each section begins with several photos of projects that I have created using the techniques described within the section. These are provided for your inspiration and do not, therefore, have any accompanying instructions.

First, we will go over some of the basic information for polymer clay. Next, I will show you some of the basics of doing "canework," or patterned clay. Then we will try using some molds and textural techniques.

Please feel free to vary the colors I suggest for projects and even the projects themselves. It is important to us in polymer clay that we teach technique not design. In this way, we can cause the greatest amount of growth in our medium. When I teach a polymer clay basics class, there is a small surprised reaction from the students about this freedom but it has its rewards. There is a time when I just sit quietly and watch. My students are empowered with the techniques I've taught them, and they are so busy adapting these techniques to their needs and tastes that they don't notice that I've ceased teaching and started learning from them!

My friends will be dropping in from time to time to add to your journey. This book is a sort of oral history of my journey on the polymer path. Shall we begin your new path?

The Goddess Polymeria by Z Kripke

Dea Polymerae, Goddess of Polymer—This spirit is especially active at night, bringing inspiration to her adherents so that they labor, knead, bake, and worship her during the all-nighter. She rewards those faithful to her with beauty, joy, and creative satisfaction. May you commune with her often.

(Make a color photocopy of this page and hang it over your clay table.)

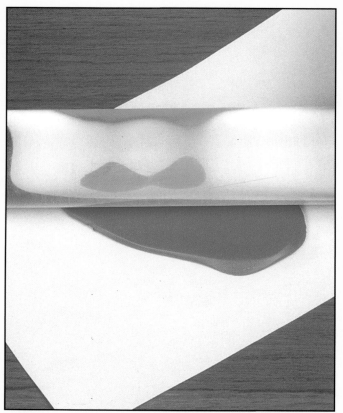

Section 1: *polymer clay basics*

What do I need to get started?

Getting Started

First, get over the idea that this is difficult. There are three things I can count on to happen in each beginning class I teach. First, everyone will be very impressed with my beads until they cut open their first canes and find themselves saying, "That's it? That's all there is to it?" Then, about midway through, they will start looking at my once impressive pile of beads and say, "Oh, okay, I see it now." And then, finally, someone will suddenly look up and announce, "That's it. I'm calling in sick to work tomorrow." Guaranteed.

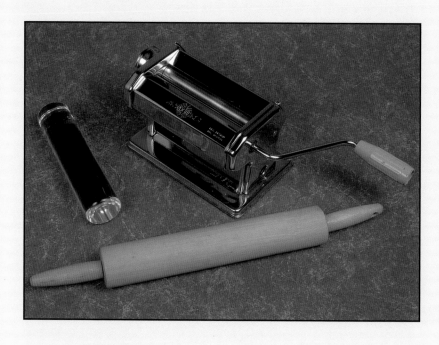

Tools

Gathering tools for working with polymer clay is quite a lot of fun and fairly inexpensive. There are some basic tools that you will use for each clay project. There are also a wide variety of additional tools available that can help you create some incredible textures and effects.

Basic Clay Tools: There are not a lot of materials needed to create with polymer clay—a few blocks of clay, something to make the clay flat, a sharp blade, a work surface, and an oven for baking. Note: Any tool or surface used for clay should not be used for food.

Tools to Flatten Clay—
    Acrylic rod
    Brayer
    Pasta machine, clay-dedicated
        (recommended)
    Rolling pin
    Wallpaper blades
    Water glass

Tools to Cut Clay—
    Craft knife
    Unimpeded edge blades for caning:
        Clay blades
        Ripple-cut blades
        Tissue blades
        Wallpaper blades

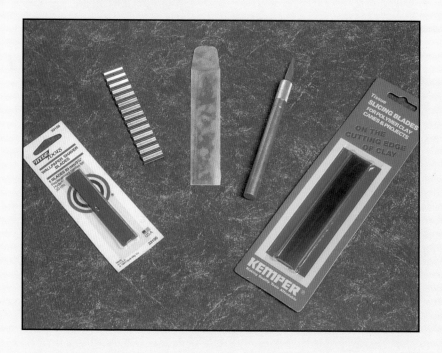

Working Surfaces—
    Acrylic sheets
    Baking parchment
    Ceramic tiles
    Drafting vellum
    File folders
    Index cards
    Poster board
    Smooth, nonporous, nonfood surfaces

Ovens—
    Convection oven
    Home oven (for occasional baking)
    Toaster oven
    NO microwave

Additional Tools: You won't find an enormous amount of items marketed specifically for clay— we borrow from all media—from painters and sculptors, to metal workers and wood workers, to our children's toy boxes and our tool boxes. Once you begin to recognize potential clay tools, the garage will never look the same to you.

Piercing Tools—large needles, small knitting needles, piercing tools, and bamboo skewers.

Jewelry Findings—Stringing materials for beadwork; regular store-bought findings for assemblage; or make your own.

Sandpaper—wet sanding to prevent dust is strongly recommended. The really high-grade sandpapers can be found at automotive stores.

Garage Tools—nails and screws for textures; pliers for assemblage; flood lights for 2 a.m. work; and burnt out light bulbs for vessel shapes.

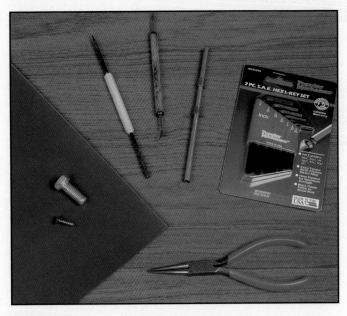

Kitchen Tools—empty jars for making covered vessels; old forks make great texture tools; and old spoons work well for braying down transfers.

Toy-box Tools—plastic dinosaurs for fossils, action figures and small dolls for hand and face molds; old crayons to chop up and mix in the clay—Lindley Hunani showed us that trick; soft-lead colored pencils to color transfers and baked clay.

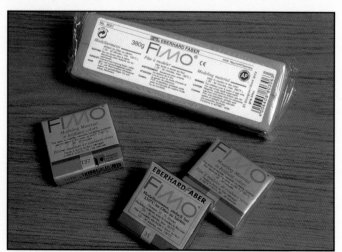

Backyard Tools—rocks, sticks, and bark for textures; sand and dirt to mix into clay; leaves for textures and molds; and dried flowers for mixing into translucent clay.

Choosing Clay

There are several brands of clay available. I will tell you from my experience with these brands of clay what I think of them.

FIMO: This is a stiff, stiff, stiff clay. Get the food processor ready for this clay. The colors are okay but reds and blues darken when baking. The tensile strength is moderate to good.

Sculpey: This is a basic modeling clay. It is chalky and very soft in its raw state. It only comes in white. Its tensile strength is not great. However, this is a good clay to paint on. It bakes very hard.

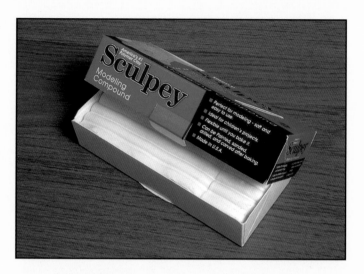

Super Sculpey: This is the darling of sculptors and doll-makers. Its tensile strength is moderate. The texture of this clay is smoother and its color is translucent beige.

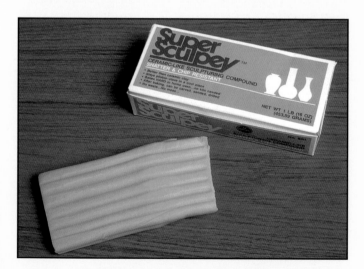

Sculpey III: This is the top children's modeling clay. It is available in great colors, very easy to work with, and its tensile strength is moderate. It is soft enough for children to use quite easily. Sculpey III bakes to a very hard surface. It is the preferred clay of my children. The Sculpey Clay

Kits for children are wonderful—the instructions include nonverbal pictures and there is plenty of clay included. If I don't give these for birthday gifts, I can expect a disappointed look from the birthday child.

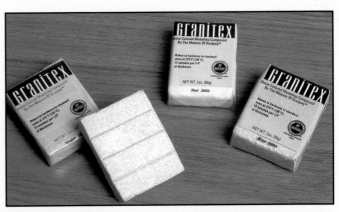

Sculpey Super Flex: We're talking pure un-adulterated fun here. This clay is flexible after it bakes. There are 50 tub toys in my bathtub that are a testament to this. It is currently available in eight colors and in kit form.

Sculpey Premo: This clay is my favorite. American polymer artists, led by my friend Marie Segal of the Clay Factory, in conjunction with the Polyform team, designed this clay. It is pasta-machine-ready and also has excellent tensile strength. It is available in wonderful colors with intense color saturation. NOW, you know why it's my favorite!

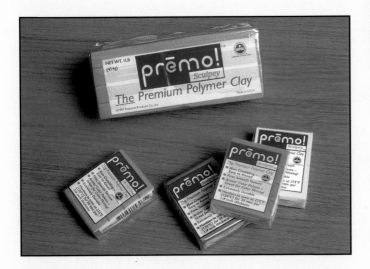

Liquid Sculpey: Oh boy, this is truly amazing stuff. It's not available on the general market, see the list of websites in the back. "LS," as it is referred to on the internet is available in opaque white and transparent. You can pour it, paint it, or drizzle it.

Sculpey Granitex: This is a material that was designed to imitate stone. It has moderate tensile strength and mixes well with Sculpey Premo. The nylon fibers in this clay preclude caning with it.

Cernit: This is another doll-maker's clay. It is a moderately stiff clay and most colors are translucent. It doesn't cane well unless mixed with other clays. Cernit and Sculpey III mixed 1:1 makes a great caning clay.

All these clays can be intermixed together. Just remember that if you do mix them for a cane, you need to keep the consistency of the clays the same throughout the cane.

Safely Using Polymer Clay

Even though the clays are AP certified non-toxic, we follow basic safety procedures for petroleum-based products:

• Any tool or surface you use for clay should not be used for food.

• Anything created or covered with clay should not be used for food or food handling.

• Wash hands after handling the clay and before eating to remove the plasticizer.

• Bake outside when possible. Ventilate interior rooms when baking inside.

• NEVER exceed recommended baking temperatures.

• Check the oven for stray clay pieces after removing baking trays.

• Be aware of repetitive-motion injuries. If you are experiencing hand or arm discomfort, PUT THE CLAY AWAY for awhile. This is particularly important when working with stiffer clays.

• Some artists wear latex gloves when handling the clay. I use them only to prevent fingerprints.

• Some of the clay pigments will come off on hands, so use lighter colors first.

• Cover, wrap, or bag the clay to keep pets and pet hair out of the clay.

Conditioning the Clay

All techniques and projects in this book call for clay that has already been conditioned and is ready to work with. All polymer clays on the market contain polymer fibers. These little fibers just love to connect with each other, providing durability and the magic of the clay. When you purchase the clay, these fibers are all jumbled up like uncombed hair. We want the fibers all smoothed out and going the same way when we use them, so we do what is called "conditioning" before we use any polymer clay. Well-conditioned clay will not have rough edges when rolled through a pasta machine and will stretch slightly before breaking when you pull on it. Soft clay is the result of conditioning—all clays need this process.

Conditioning the clay by hand: Cut the clay block in half, then cut each half into three pieces. Begin rolling one of these pieces into a ball, roll into a snake, fold it in half to form a ball, and repeat until the clay feels flexible and it stretches.

Conditioning the clay using a clay-dedicated pasta machine: Cut slices off the block of clay. Roll a slice through the pasta machine. Fold the clay in half and roll it through again, folded side first to force the air out. As each piece becomes workable, add another piece off the block.

Conditioning the clay using a clay-dedicated food processor: Fortunately the newer clays have allowed us to do without this method. But if you have some particularly stiff clay, chop it up and put it into a clay-dedicated food processor or chopper and whirl away. You may even add a few drops of mineral oil, baby oil, or diluent to help soften the clay. Clay conditioned in a food processor looks like cottage cheese. When conditioned this way and pressed into small balls, turquoise clay resembles stone nuggets.

Conditioned clay will maintain its flexibility for several hours and will remain more flexible than unconditioned clay for several days.

Rolling Sheets of Clay
This should be titled "I'm going to tell you everything it took me months to figure out about a pasta machine."

Rolling the clay out by hand: Always work on a nonporous surface so you can peel the clay up. Baking parchment, drafting vellum, index cards, and file folders all work well.

Begin by rolling the clay in all four directions with a flattening tool. I have used acrylic rods, water glasses, and books. Experiment until you find what works best in each situation.

If you are going to create a very thin sheet of clay, "sandwich" the clay between drafting vellum or baking parchment.

Note: Go slowly! The clay will stick to work and tool surfaces if you try to press down too much.

Rolling the clay using a pasta machine: Remember that if you use the machine for clay, it is dedicated to this medium. Do not make pasta with it after using it for clay.

Use a manual pasta machine. A motor can be attached to it later if you wish.

We like to use a pasta machine imported from Italy. It has seven to nine thickness settings on it. The settings are adjustable with the dial on the side.

We typically refer to the settings as they are numbered, #1 being the thickest and #7 the thinnest.

Start with a #1 setting and then move to the smaller settings. This will keep the clay in a workable squared size and shape.

Make certain to roll the clay through the pasta machine folded side first to force out air.

Note: I do not clean the pasta machine. I just run scrap clay through it before rolling a critical color, such as white. All the other little bits of color just mix in.

For the Sake of Reference
I thought it might be convenient to show you exactly the width of the sheets I will be talking about in these projects. For the sake of expediency, I usually refer to the sheets by the number on the pasta machine that makes that particular width.

#1 or ⅛"

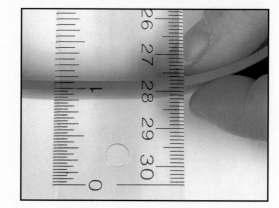

#2 or ³⁄₃₂"

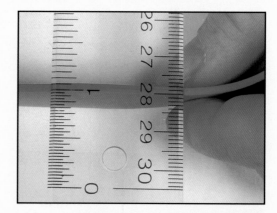

#3 or ¹⁄₁₆"

#4 or ³⁄₆₄"

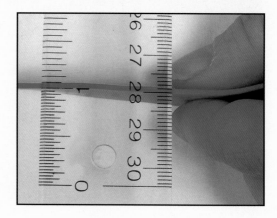

#5 or ¹⁄₃₂"

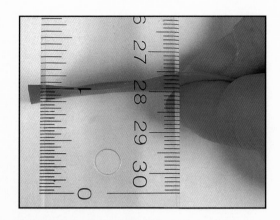

I tend to use numbers #1, #3, and #5 the most. If you are using a pasta machine, you may want to compare the sheets your machine makes to mine as they can differ from one machine to another by as much as one sheet thickness.

PLEASE NOTE THAT ALL PROJECTS ARE USING CONDITIONED CLAY AND A PASTA MACHINE.

Troubleshooting with Clay
Here are some helpful hints just in case you should run into any problems when working with polymer clay.

Clay is too hard: A plasticizer or diluent can be added to soften the clay. Chop up the clay and add just a few drops of mineral oil, baby oil, or diluent to the clay. Allow the clay to sit for one hour before mixing.

Clay is too soft: Soft clay can be "leached" to remove some of the excess plasticizer. Place sheets of clay between layers of absorbent paper like blank newsprint or simply leave the package open for a couple of days.

Clay just keeps crumbling: Remember that both heat and ultraviolet rays will affect the clay. Do not leave the clay in the car all day, on top of the oven, or in front of a window. Also, buy only from a reputable source that has handled and stored the clay correctly. I once walked into a bead store, which had its clay selection displayed in the front window. I never went back.

Clay turns dark in the oven: Check the baking temperature and do a test piece again. You may be scorching the clay.

Need green clay but don't have any: Do you have blue and yellow clays? Do not be afraid to mix your own colors. Buy a color-mixing chart or take a color theory class if you just cannot figure out that ecru is three parts white and one part raw sienna.

Baking the Clay
The clay must be properly baked to complete the polymerization process. There are lots of opinions on just how to achieve this. I use the technique that my friend and mentor, Marie Segal, has devised. She was instrumental in the formulation of the Sculpey Premo clay and she is a wealth of information about polymer clay.

1. Check the baking temperature of your oven with a thermometer. Does it bake hotter or cooler than indicated temperature? Adjust the suggested starting temperature accordingly.

2. Place a sheet of conditioned clay, rolled on #1, on a piece of baking parchment, an index card, or a file folder.

19

3. Place the clay and the paper on a clay-dedicated cookie sheet and place them in a cold oven.

4. Turn the oven to 200° for 10 minutes. This allows the entire piece to heat to an even temperature before polymerization of the surfaces.

5. After 10 minutes, turn the oven up to 275°, adjusted according to your oven thermometer, for 15 more minutes.

6. Turn the oven off and allow the piece to cool in the oven.

7. When the piece is cool, the polymerization process will be complete. You should be able to bend the piece and flex it a reasonable amount without cracking or breaking it.

Note: The baking times will vary according to the thickness of the piece. Thicker pieces will require more baking time. Check your oven frequently.

Baking Tips

Always bake the clay in a well-ventilated room. There should be a mild plastic odor when it bakes. If it starts to become bitter smelling, it is probably scorching or burning.

If you are baking large areas of white clay, tent them with foil—just like you would tent a turkey—to keep the white areas from scorching.

Items can be rebaked. In fact, many of the more complex techniques require several bakings.

Whenever possible, allow the pieces to cool in the oven. This is especially important with pieces that have a lot of bulk to them. Cracks can appear in the outside layers of clay if large items are not cooled slowly. If small cracks occur, put them back into a warm oven. The cracks often close on their own.

If you are baking in your home oven and you are concerned about the fumes there is a simple method of containment:

1. Purchase two foil roasting pans (the same size).

2. Line one roasting pan with some file folders or index cards and place the pieces inside.

3. Place the remaining roasting pan upside down on top of the first pan. Clip them closed with sturdy clothespins or gator clips.

4. Bake.

5. When the pans have cooled enough to touch, take them outside and remove the clips. The clay will be baked and the fumes will not be inside your house.

Making Basic Canes

Polymer canework has its roots in millifiore glass beadwork. Essentially, you are creating a one-dimensional picture or pattern in three dimensions. When you make the cane smaller (we call this "reducing the cane"), those polymer fibers will slip on themselves and retain the pattern. Once the pattern is created and reduced to the dimension you want it to be, you can slice the cane like slicing cookie dough and use the pieces for beads or for decorating other items. The pattern is created on the INSIDE and you do not see it until you cut the cane open.

There are five basic patterns to canework. Clockwise from left, they are the bull's eye, the Skinner blend, the banner, the pinroll, and the checkerboard.

Reducing & Reshaping a Cane

Good technique for cane reduction forces all the layers of clay to move at once and reduces distortion and waste. There are as many techniques for cane reduction as there are canes. Marie Segal showed me the following method.

To reduce a round cane:

1. Pick the cane up in the middle with your left hand. Place it in the area between your right thumb and forefinger and wrap your remaining fingers around the bottom half of the cane.

2. Now squeeze. Move your hands up the cane and squeeze again.

3. When you get to the top, turn the cane over. Starting at the middle, begin squeezing. Repeat in this manner to end of the cane. Note: I know it looks a mess now, but remember the magic is inside.

4. Roll the cane on the work surface to smooth it out and reduce it a little more to the largest diameter desired.

To reshape and reduce a square cane:
1. Convert a round cane to a square by pressing on all four sides of the round cane to create a square shape.

2. Using the lengths of your thumbs and forefingers, squeeze in the middle and squeeze out to each end. Note: Square canes are easier to cut without distortion than round canes.

3. Use an acrylic rod or brayer to even the sides and sharpen the edges.

To reshape and reduce a triangular cane:
1. Convert a round cane to a triangular cane, beginning with the round cane slightly larger than you want the finished cane.

2. Set the cane on the table and pinch up one side of the cane.

3. Roll the cane over, and pinch up the other two sides.

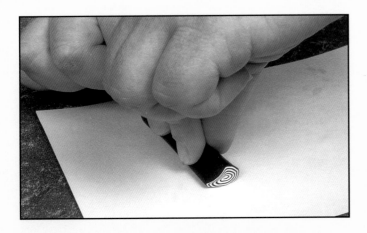

4. Smooth out the edges of the triangle by sliding your fingers down the cane from the middle to the edges. This will also help reduce the cane.

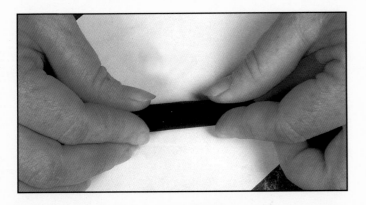

To reshape and reduce an oval cane:
1. Reduce the round cane to the size desired for the oval cane.

2. Using an acrylic rod or brayer, lightly roll down the top of the cane to flatten it into an oval.

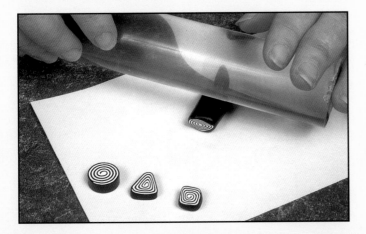

Allowing the Clay to Rest

As mentioned previously, the softness of the clay is enhanced as a result of the conditioning process. Climate, temperature, and the warmth of your hands are also factors. Once you build a cane, it is recommended to allow the cane to "rest" for 15–30 minutes unless specified otherwise. This time allows the fibers to re-create their contacts and the fillers and binders to solidify once again. Resting also allows for cleaner cuts and less distortion in the pattern of the cane.

Using Molds

If canework causes you to see images in a different way, wait until you play with molds. Ready-made molds are available for purchase in crafts stores. However, we can also make our own original molds at home. We make molds of almost everything. Note: When making molds it is important to remember artist ethics and honor any applicable copyrights.

Simple Molds: Use scrap clay as the mold material. The mold masters, Judi Maddigan and Maureen Carlson, suggest forming the clay into a soft point and placing the point of clay into the deepest part of the mold. Note: Both Judi and Maureen have excellent websites listed as links of the San Diego Guild website.

Premo Sculpey clay seems to have a "memory" for detail. Use a mold of unbaked Premo for the impression if you are in a hurry or do not want a permanent mold. Katherine Dewey showed me this little trick one year in Dallas.

Mold Release: A mold release is used to protect the original item being molded. The mold release is also used to help keep the clay being molded from sticking to the mold. Use baby powder, water, or a petroleum-based vinyl protectant as common mold releases. Apply the release agent to either the mold or the surface of the clay to be molded.

Using Rubber Stamps with Polymer Clay

Rubber stamps work very well with this medium. Look for well-defined images on the stamps to create fairly deep impressions.

Use a mold release to protect the stamps and aid in achieving a clean impression.

Heat-set inks work superbly with the clay. If you have not used these inks before, they are inks that do not "set" until heat is applied. Thus, you can cure the clay and set the ink in one baking.

The inks can be embossed into the surface or stamped onto the smooth surface of the clay.

Nancy Babb sent me this fabulous pin, using heat-set ink and stamps.

Using Translucent Heat-embossing Powders with Polymer Clay

Remember that a little of these powders goes a long way. You can use your fingers to apply these powders directly to the raw clay.

A small paintbrush can be used to create a soft layer of the powders, but the paintbrush does not control the powder very well, so be very careful.

My favorite tool for applying the powder is a small rubber sculpting chisel. This little tool allows you to "paint" the surface of the clay and create a straight line of powder.

This translucent heat-embossing powder can be applied to the raw surface of the clay before baking. It also can be mixed into the clays for a very subtle metallic effect.

This powder also can be mixed into a surface sealant, resulting in a lovely glistening effect that is perfect for leaves and fairies.

Sanding Polymer Clay

Always use wet sandpaper and sand under water as much as possible. My expert, Jami Miller, says to soak the sandpaper for at least an hour before use.

The most common grits are the very high-end grits—300, 400, and higher. You can use a few of the lower grits if you need to take a lot off the surface right away. The very high-end grits are available at auto parts stores for car painting.

Begin with the lowest grit and sand in all four directions for at least one to two minutes. Continue this process with each higher grit. The finer grit you use, the better the finish will be.

Polymer clay can be polished on a polishing wheel after sanding. Use only a muslin wheel and no polishing paste.

This beautiful necklace was made by Dottie McMillan and was sanded and polished after baking. The jade was created of mostly translucent clay with a little green, burnt ochre, and purple.

Finishing Polymer Clay
Sealants for Polymer Clay: There are sealants, called glazes, available for finishing or sealing the clay.

I prefer to use a water-based varathane in the clear satin finish. It has no smell and it is nearly invisible on the surface of the clay. Take care not to apply too much in one coat as it can cause a milky effect.

Some floor waxes are polymer-based products that can be rubbed or brushed onto the surface. You can also dip the whole piece like these large molded beads I made.

Antiquing Polymer Clay: There are many ways to "antique" the surface of the clay. We have used brown acrylic paint in several projects.

Marie Segal made this lovely pendant by painting the entire surface with heat-set ink, curing it, and then sanding off the surface, producing a neat inlay of pigment without any residual pigment on the upper layers.

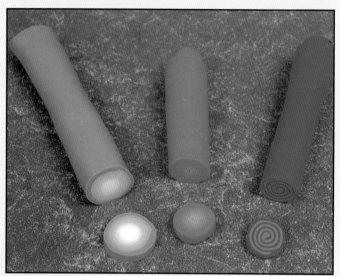

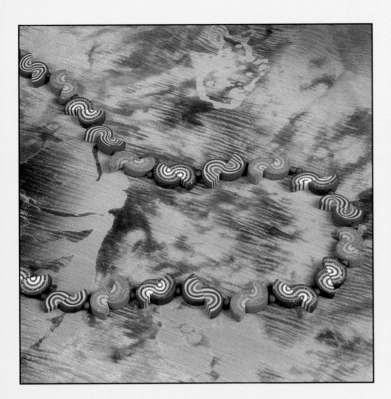

Section 2: *basic canes*

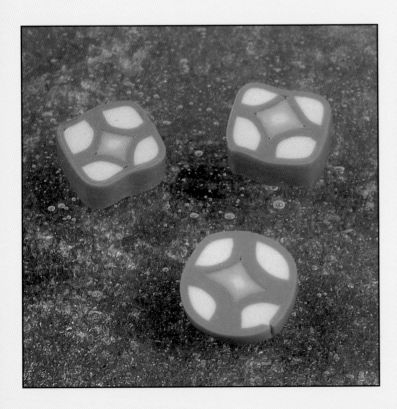

1
basic canes

How do I make a pinroll cane?

What You Need to Get Started:

Basic clay tools
Glass candle-
  holder
Sculpey Premo
  clay in 2 oz.
  packages:
  black (1);
  white (1)

The pinroll is perfect for covering a small candleholder. Give new life to an older candleholder or embellish a new plain glass candleholder. I often make these and fill them with matching beads. They make excellent gifts for the creative people on my gift lists.

Small Candleholder

Here's How:

1. Roll a #1 sheet from ½ package of the white clay.

2. Cut the biggest rectangle possible from this sheet of clay.

3. Repeat Step 1 with ½ package of the black clay.

4. Place the white rectangle on the black and trim the edges to match.

5. Place the sandwiched rectangle of clay with the black side down. This will make the outside layer of the pinroll black.

6. Trim the two short ends of the rectangle to 45°, so that the white layer is slightly shorter than the black.

7. Pinch up one of the short ends and slowly roll the rectangle up. Push the ends back into the cane as they spread out.

8. Gently roll the cane on the work surface to seal the outside.

9. Refer to Reducing & Reshaping a Cane on page 21. Reduce the cane to the first desired size. Allow the cane to rest for 10–15 minutes.

10. Cut the cane for the first time right in the middle, as this should produce the least distorted image.

11. Cut thin slices from the cane.

12. Gently press the slices evenly into place around the upper edge of the candleholder.

13. Repeat Steps 11–12 for the bottom edge of the candleholder.

14. Using a water glass or acrylic rod, press and smooth the slices into place.

15. Refer to Baking the Clay on page 19. Bake the covered candleholder. Allow to cool. Note: The clay will adhere to the glass without adhesives. However, if you decide you don't like the configuration or just wish to change it after baking, just peel the clay off.

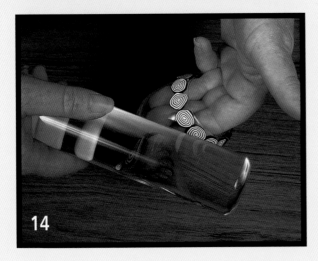

29

2
basic canes

How do I resize and reshape a pinroll cane?

Remember, once you create a cane, you can resize and reshape all of it or portions of it for different uses. I have the habit of saving portions of cane for later use. Earrings make quick and easy small projects to start your new jewelry collection. You can make them as simple or elaborate as you wish. Wait until you see the reaction of your friends when you wear them.

Earrings

Here's How:

1. Refer to Reducing & Reshaping a Cane on page 21. Reduce ¼ of the cane to ¼" diameter.

2. Cut two ¼"-thick slices from the cane.

3. Reshape the rest of the cane to form a triangle.

4. Cut two ¼"-thick slices from the triangular cane.

5. Using the needle tool, pierce each bead by twisting it halfway through the bead. Complete the pierce from the other side of the bead.

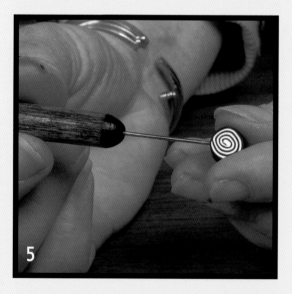

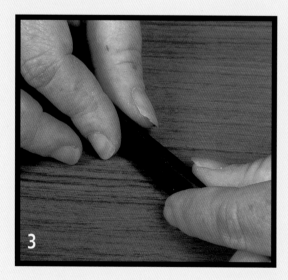

6. For coordinating beads, form some small balls and some flattened balls from the contrasting color of clay and pierce them.

7. Refer to Baking the Clay on page 19. Bake the beads. Allow to cool.

8. Place the beads on the T-pin as desired.

9. Using the pliers, trim the T-pin to ¼" longer than the stack of beads.

10. Grip the top of the T-pin. Roll the pliers to form a circle.

11. Thread the French loop wire on and close the loop.

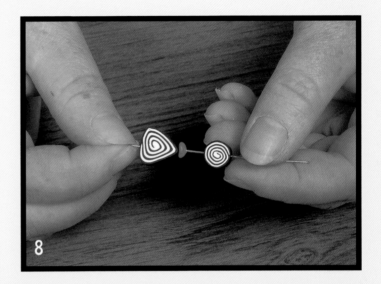

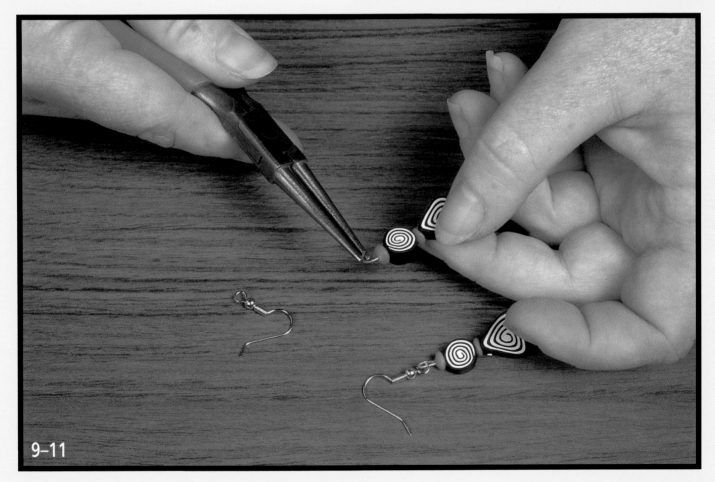

3
basic canes

How do I recombine the pinroll cane?

What You Need to Get Started:

Basic clay tools
Napkin rings:
  ceramic, metal,
  or wood
Sculpey Premo clay
  in 2 oz.
  packages:
  ultramarine blue
  (1); turquoise (1)

The complexity of millefiori canes is created by the combination and recombination of basic patterns. This project is an excellent demonstration of using basic patterns to create a lovely new life for an old set of napkin rings.

Napkin Rings

Here's How:
1. Refer to Steps 1–8 for Basic Canes 1 on page 28. Make a pinroll cane from ultramarine blue and turquoise clays.

2. Refer to Reducing & Reshaping a Cane on page 21. Reduce the pinroll cane to ½" diameter. Allow the cane to rest 20–30 minutes.

3. Cut the cane into four equal pieces.

4. Stack the four cane pieces together to make a square.

5. Roll a small long snake from the turquoise clay. Cut the snake into five equal pieces. Place one piece in the intersection of the four canes.

6. Place remaining snake pieces in the outside intersections of the canes. This creates a Spanish tile effect. Gently press the pieces together.

7. Reduce for a square cane. We now have an intricate design from our simple pinrolls.

8. Cut thin slices from the cane.

9. Press the slices onto the outside of the napkin rings.

10. Using an acrylic rod, smooth the cane slices in place, taking care not to smear the designs.

11. Refer to Baking the Clay on page 19. Bake the napkin rings. Allow to cool.

4
basic canes

How do I turn the pinroll cane inside out?

What You Need to Get Started:

Basic clay tools
Necklace clasp
Needle tool: long, thin
Round-nosed pliers
Sculpey Premo clay in 2 oz. packages: black (1); ecru (1); gold (1)
Stringing material
T-pin and French loop wire for earring assembly

Two of my favorite people showed me two of my favorite techniques. Marie Segal showed me the Inside-out cane technique and Mike Buessler showed me how to create the Mobius bead. Both techniques work with almost any cane pattern, but I prefer them with this particular pattern.

Mobius Bead

Here's How:

1. Refer to Steps 1–8 for Basic Canes 1 on page 28. Make two pinroll canes from black and ecru clays.

2. Refer to Reducing & Reshaping a Cane on page 21. Reduce the pinroll canes to ½" diameter. Allow the canes to rest 20–30 minutes.

3. Cut one cane right in the middle. Cut one piece of the cane in half lengthwise.

4. Cut these two halves lengthwise again, creating quarters of the original cane.

5. Reassemble these pieces inside out.

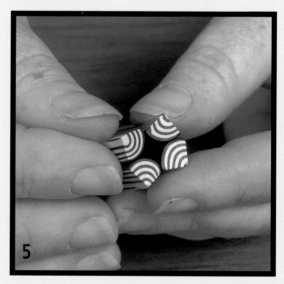

6. Roll a snake from the gold clay. Place the snake in the center of the four cane pieces to fill the area. Gently press the pieces together.

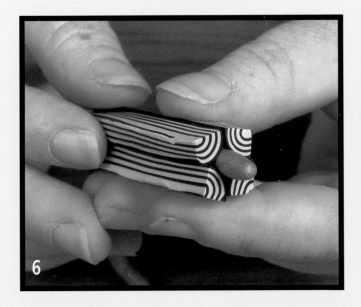

7. Roll a #5 sheet from the remaining black clay.

8. Place the cane pieces on the black sheet of clay. Trim the sheet of clay behind one long edge of the cane. Trim up the two sides of the sheet, using the ends of the cane as a guide.

9. Roll the cane pieces up in the black clay until the edges touch. Roll it back slightly and look at the surface of the black clay. There will be a dent where the leading edge of the black clay touched itself. Trim the black clay at the dent. Lightly roll the cane on the work surface to seal the wrap.

10. Reduce for a ¾"-square cane.

11. Cut several thin (less than ⅛") slices from the cane. Set aside some slices for filler beads.

12. Make Mobius beads by holding two opposite corners of one slice with your right thumb and forefinger. The slice should look diamond shaped between your two fingers.

13. Reach from behind the slice and touch the two opposite corners with your left thumb and forefinger.

14. Gently pull your two hands apart while folding the opposite corners toward each other. You have now created a wonderful three-dimensional shape that looks like an animal print. Allow the beads to rest for a few minutes.

15. Repeat Steps 12–14 for number of Mobius beads desired.

16. Make round filler beads of consistent size, by rolling a snake first and cutting it into equal sized pieces. Roll each piece into a ball.

17. Cut several slices from the remaining pinroll cane for filler beads.

18. Using the needle tool, pierce each filler bead and each Mobius bead by twisting it halfway through the bead. Complete the pierce from the other side of the bead, resealing the points of the Mobius beads as they are pierced.

19. Refer to Baking the Clay on page 19. Bake the beads. Allow to cool.

20. Refer to Steps 8–11 for Basic Canes 2 on page 30. Place beads as desired for earrings.

21. Place the beads onto stringing material to length desired.

22. Attach necklace clasp to ends of stringing material to create a necklace.

Design Tips:

The Mobius beads work best with a fresh cane that is still well-conditioned. If the points come apart, apply a dot of super strength craft adhesive to seal them.

A pinroll does not have to be just two colors—try three colors rolled together.

Try making the layers rolled together different thicknesses.

Use a very thin layer of a lighter color or white to separate two dark colors.

Try mixing embossing powder into the clays before making the pinrolls. The embossing powders will "bloom" when they are baked. They will show more when baked, so remember, a little goes a long way. Mix lighter colored powders into darker clays and darker colored powders into lighter clays. My favorite Mobius bead is made up of dark blue clay with white embossing powder pinrolled with white clay that is mixed with dark blue embossing powder.

Pinrolls recombined together do not have to be from the same cane. Use complementary or contrasting colored canes together.

Inside-out canes do not have to be from the same cane. Mix and match was never so fun.

5
basic canes

How do I make a bull's eye cane?

Bull's eye canes are the most creative of the basic canes. They can be simple or elaborate, bold or subtly colored. The frame project described here has become one of my favorite creations. I now have little bull's eye frames all over the house and I'm considering making a bull's eye "frame" for my computer monitor

What You Need to Get Started:

Acrylic frame:
  clear, small
Basic clay tools
Index cards (2)
Sculpey Premo
  clay in 2 oz.
  packages: black
  (2); fuchsia (1);
  green (1);
  orange (1)

Clay Frame

Here's How:
1. Roll a little less than half of the fuchsia clay into a ball. Elongate the ball into a 1½"- to 2"-long cylinder.

2. Roll a #1 sheet from half of the black clay. Roll a #5 sheet from this sheet of clay.

3. Refer to Steps 8–9 for Basic Canes 4 on page 34. Wrap the fuchsia cylinder with the sheet of black clay. Note: The resulting cane is called a bull's eye.

5. Roll another #5 sheet from the black clay. Wrap it around the bull's eye cane.

6. Roll a #3 sheet from the orange clay. Wrap it around the bull's eye cane.

7. Finally, roll another #5 sheet from the black clay. Wrap it around the bull's eye cane. Roll the cane on the work surface to seal the wraps.

4. Roll a #3 sheet from the green clay. Wrap it around the bull's eye cane.

8. Refer to Reducing & Reshaping a Cane on page 21. Reduce the bull's eye cane to ¾" diameter.

9. Cut the cane right in the middle and reduce one piece to ½" diameter. Allow the cane to rest for at least 30 minutes.

10. Roll a #3 sheet from the remaining black clay. Place the acrylic frame, face down, on the sheet of clay.

11. Cut the clay slightly larger than the frame to allow for minimal shrinkage.

12. Cut one index card to form a template the size of the photo area of the frame. Center this on the black clay and cut around the edge of the index card. This will form the clay frame background of the project. Keep the clay frame on the index card.

16. Glue the clay frame onto the acrylic frame.

13. Cut thin slices from the cane and place them randomly on the clay frame.

14. Embellish the clay frame further with little dots of fuchsia, green, and orange clays.

15. Refer to Baking the Clay on page 19. Place the decorated clay frame on the second index card and bake, taking care to keep the frame flat. Allow to cool. Note: The acrylic frame does not go in the oven.

6
basic canes

What You Need to Get Started:

Basic clay tools
Colored glass
   ornament
Sculpey Premo
   clay in 2 oz.
   packages:
   translucent (1);
   white (1)

How do I use the bull's eye cane?

Create a special project using the bull's eye cane. This is a fun project to do with your children for the holidays. It is an excellent way to hide scratches and flaws in older ornaments.

Lacy Ornament

Here's How:
1. Refer to Basic Canes 1 on page 28. Make a pinroll cane from the white and translucent clays, using ½ a package of each color.

2. Refer to Reducing & Reshaping a Cane on page 21. Reduce the cane to ¼" diameter.

3. Cut the cane right in the middle. Reduce one piece to a smaller diameter.

4. Refer to Steps 1–3 for Basic Canes 5 on page 38. Roll a cylinder from the remaining translucent clay. Roll a #1 sheet from white clay. Wrap the sheet of white clay around the cylinder to make a bull's eye cane.

5. Reduce this cane to ¼" diameter. Cut the cane into three equal pieces. Cut two of the pieces into smaller dimensions and reduce them to smaller diameters. Allow the canes to rest at least one hour. Note: The end result should be two patterns in various small sizes.

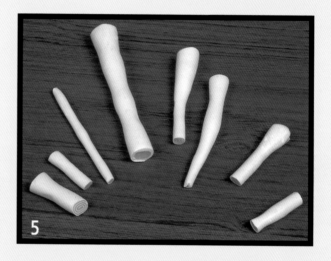

6. Cut very thin slices from the canes. Varying the sizes and patterns, press the slices onto the top of the ornament just below the hanger to create a random lace effect down from the top of the ornament.

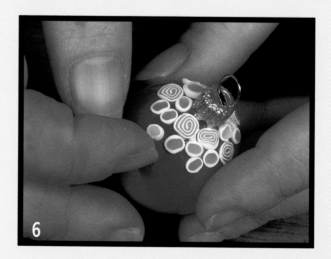

7. Refer to Baking the Clay on page 19. Bake the ornament. Allow to cool. Note: The translucent quality of the clay will allow the original color of the ornament to show through the canes.

Design Tips:

If you have a star cutter, try cutting some of the pinrolls with the cutter.

This is also a great pattern for covering vases. Cover the bottom and around the top rim of a cocktail juice bottle to hold cut roses.

7
basic canes

How do I add a banner to the bull's eye cane?

What You Need to Get Started:

Basic clay tools
Needle tool: large
Phillips screw-
    driver: small
Premade bull's
    eye cane: 2"
    long, ¾"
    diameter
Sculpey Premo
    clay in 2 oz.
    packages:
    colors used for
    the bull's eye (⅓
    package each);
    black, ecru, or
    white (⅓
    package)

The banner technique is a quick and easy way to achieve a striping effect. I like to use the technique for making buttons. Made from Sculpey Premo polymer clay, they are very sturdy; they can withstand many cycles through the washer and dryer. Years ago, I made buttons for a denim shirt I have. The denim has now faded with all the washings, but the buttons are still pristine.

Buttons

Here's How:

1. Roll clay colors, including those used in the bull's eye cane, into balls.

2. Flatten the clay balls into little "pillow" shapes. Note: The pillows do not need to be the same thickness, but roughly the same shape and size.

3. Stack the pillows on top of each other, alternating the contrasting light and black color, if desired.

4. Slightly press the stack together and cut in half.

5. Restack the two halves on top of each other. Set the stack on the work surface and press it out to the same size you began with. This will have the effect of compressing the layers together.

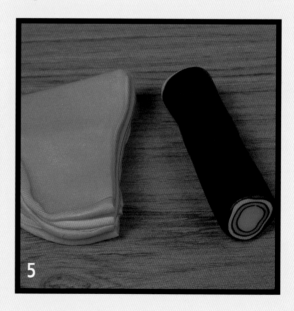

6. Cut the stack in half and repeat Step 5.

7. Cut the stack in half again. Observe that the layers are now fine stripes of color. Note: The intricacy of the striping is controlled by the number of times Steps 4–5 are repeated.

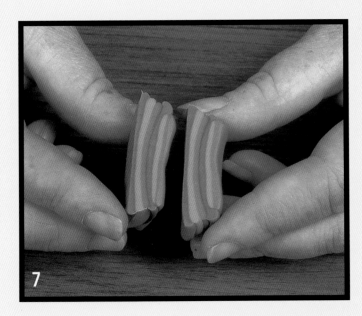

8. Compare the stack to the bull's eye cane. Select the side of the stack that most closely matches the length of the cane. Cut ⅛"-thick slices of the stack.

9. Place these slices around the outside edge of the cane, alternating the striping and allowing the slices to touch but not overlap. Trim the last slice lengthwise to fit, if necessary.

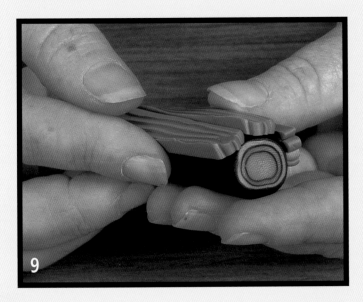

10. Gently roll the cane on the work surface to seal. Slightly reduce the cane.

11. Cut the cane right in the middle. At this point, add a thin wrap of color to the outside if desired. Allow the cane to rest 15–20 minutes.

12. Cut ³⁄₁₆"- to ¼"-thick slices from the cane to make buttons. If desired, round the edges of the buttons with your finger.

13. Using the large needle tool or a phillips screwdriver, create the thread holes. Angle the holes toward the outside to help strengthen the thread and button.

14. Refer to Baking the Clay on page 19. Bake the buttons. Allow to cool.

8
basic canes

**What You Need
to Get Started:**

Basic clay tools
Leftover banner
  cane
Necklace clasp
Needle tool: long
Sculpey Premo
  clay: colors of
  the banner
  cane (scraps)
Stringing material

How do I use the banner cane?

The uneven striping effect created by the banner technique perfectly yields itself to wonderful twisted beads. These beads are great when alternated with coordinating pinroll beads. Made into a piece of jewelry, they would be just right to wear with a pair of striped pants.

Twisted Beads

Here's How:
1. Cut a ¼"-thick slice from the leftover banner cane.

2. Evenly twist the slice.

3. Cut the twist into desired lengths.

4. Roll small balls from the solid colors of clay. Press them onto the ends of the twists, making end caps and completing the beads.

5. Using the needle tool, pierce each bead by twisting it halfway through the bead. Complete the pierce from the other side of the bead.

6. Refer to Baking the Clay on page 19. Bake the beads. Allow to cool.

7. Refer to Steps 21–22 for Basic Canes 4 on page 34. Place the beads onto stringing material to length desired and attach necklace clasp to create a necklace.

Design Tips:

Place long beads made in this fashion on either side of a large round center bead in a necklace.

Shorter beads made in this fashion look best when placed along the neckline of the necklace, interspaced with round filler beads.

Use this technique to imitate virtually any wood type. The colors you choose depend on the wood effect you want. You can even add knotholes.

If you wish the wood to look rough, texture the top of it and the sides with the blade.

Here is the entire totem pole necklace. I built this on a Fourth of July, in my driveway with my friends. I used only a linoleum tile to work on.

Even though my friends were present during the entire process, they could not believe I had "put" that fish inside.

9
basic canes

How do I make a feather cane?

What You Need to Get Started:

Basic clay tools
Postage stamps:
 Native
 American or
 Western series
Sculpey Premo
 clay in 2 oz.
 packages: black
 (1); raw sienna
 (1); white (1)
Seed beads:
 multicolored
Texturing tool
Tweezers

Here we use a cane to dress up an inexpensive and ordinary postage stamp. Once you start using postage stamps for these collages, you just can't stop. Can you imagine what my postal worker must think when I come in and say, "Please give me the ugliest stamps you have."?

Postage Stamp Collage

Here's How:

1. Roll a #3 sheet from both black and white clays.

2. Cut a 1¼" square from the black sheet of clay.

3. Place the black square on the white sheet of clay and trim to match.

4. Repeat Steps 2–3, alternating between the black and white clays until you have six layers or a square block of alternating layers of color. Note: The top and bottom layers must be different colors.

5. Gently press the stack together. Do not use too much pressure. Place the stack so the layers are perpendicular to the table.

6. Cut through the stack at an angle, making ⅛"-thick slices.

7. Stack two slices, inverting one so the lines are pointing down and matching up the colors of the stripes to create a herringbone effect.

7-8

8. Place a #5 sheet of black clay at the top third of the feather. Press the two slices together.

9. Make a small triangle from black clay. Place the triangle in the gap created at the bottom of the two slices.

10. Reduce the cane in your hands by pressing on it and pulling it slightly.

11. Cut several "feather" slices and shape them by hand to ½" long.

12. Roll a small #1 sheet from the raw sienna clay and trim it to the size desired.

13. Moisten the postage stamp and press it onto the clay. Using an acrylic rod, bray it down.

14. Using the texturing tool, texture the exposed clay around the stamp.

15. Place feather slices onto the clay as desired. Using tweezers, place the seed beads onto the clay. When you are certain of their position, carefully bray them into place.

16. Refer to Baking the Clay on page 19. Bake the postage stamp collage. Allow to cool.

9

11

10
basic canes

How do I make a checkerboard cane?

What You Need to Get Started:

Basic clay tools
Pen: round with black ink
Pliers
Sculpey Premo clay in 2 oz. packages: black (1); white (1)

There are many ways of making a checkerboard cane, but this method creates the cleanest pattern. The technique for covering pens can be used with any cane or combination of canes.

Covered Pen

Here's How:

1. Roll a #1 sheet from black and white clays.

2. Cut a 1¼" square from the black sheet of clay.

3. Place the black square on the white sheet and trim to match.

4. Repeat Steps 2–3, alternating between the black and white clays until you have six layers or a square block of alternating layers of color. Note: The top and bottom layers must be different colors.

5. Gently press the stack together. Do not use too much pressure as this could disturb the precision of the layers.

6. Turn the stack on its side so the layers are now vertical.

7. Carefully cut ⅛"-thick slices from the stacked clay. Note: I sometimes cool my stack in the refrigerator before beginning this step.

8. Flip every other slice and restack, taking care to line up the top and bottom of the cane. The colored squares should alternate into a checkerboard.

9. Refer to Reducing & Reshaping a Cane on page 21. Reduce for a square cane to ½" diameter.

10. Using a pair of pliers, remove the ink cartridge from the pen.

11. Cut thin slices from the checkerboard cane.

12. Press the slices around the barrel of the pen, avoiding overlapping the slices, but trimming them to fit. The thinness of the slices will determine the finished diameter of the pen.

13. Slowly roll the covered pen barrel on the work surface to seal the canes together.

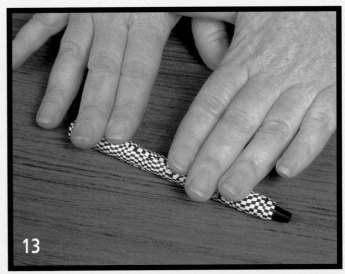

14. Trim the bottom edge of the clay to the end cap of the pen.

15. Pull the top edges together and pinch to cover the top of the pen.

16. Refer to Baking the Clay on page 19. Bake the covered pen for 20 minutes. Allow to cool.

17. Replace the ink cartridge after the pen has cooled.

Troubleshooting:
This type pen can withstand the heat of the oven quite well, while the styrene, or clear plastic pens cannot. If you have a pen you would like to cover, remove the ink from it and put it in the oven at 275° for a few minutes to determine if it will be applicable.

Design Tip:
Another method for covering the pen is to collage the slices onto a #5 sheet of scrap clay. Cover the clay with vellum or parchment and roll with an acrylic rod or brayer to blend the edges of the canes.

Design Tips (cont.):

Refer to Steps 8–9 for Basic Canes 4 on page 34. Wrap the finished piece of clay around the barrel of the pen as you would wrap a sheet around a cane. Roll the pen on the work surface to seal the wrap and smooth the clay on the barrel.

Form a holder for the pen from a ball of scrap clay, covered in canes, and rolled to seal the edges of the cane. Form the ball into a pleasing shape. Press a pen, with its ink cartridge intact, into the clay at an angle that will support the weight of the pen. Bake the clay with the pen. Allow to cool.

Do not miss the incredible mechanical pens that Jami Miller has created in the Gallery on page 106.

How do I make a blended cane using the Skinner method?

Judith Skinner told Marie Segal and I one "clay day" that she knew there had to be a simple mathematical formula for gradating colors. She showed us the technique she had devised. After we picked our chins up off the floor, we congratulated her for radically reforming the caning process. We couldn't wipe the smiles off our faces or the goosebumps off our arms.

I never do this technique without thanking Judith, whether I'm talking to a roomful of people or my cats in the garage.

What You Need to Get Started:

Basic clay tools
Brass light switch cover
Needle tool: large
Sculpey Premo clay in 2 oz. packages: cobalt blue (1); fluorescent green (1); white (3)

Light Switch Cover

Here's How:
1. Roll a #1 sheet from the blue and white clays.

2. Cut a triangle from the blue sheet of clay.

3. Cut a matching triangle from the white sheet of clay.

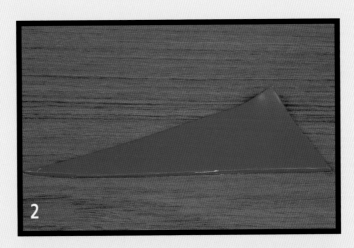

4. Place the two triangles together to form a rectangle. Press the edges together to help hold the two pieces of clay together.

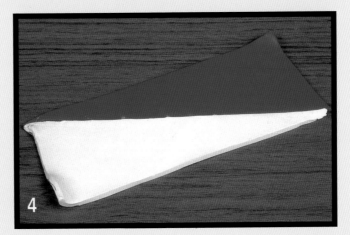

51

5. Fold the clays lengthwise and roll a #1 sheet. Keep folding and rolling, the SAME way. It takes several passes through the machine to get a nice blend. Note: At first it appears that you have just created a mess, but do not give up. You determine when the blend is sufficient.

6. Turn the blended sheet 90° and roll a #5 sheet.

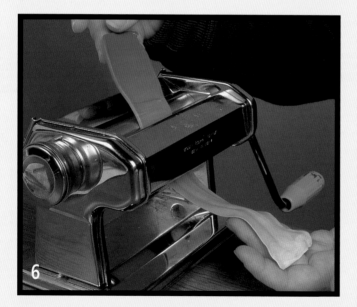

7. Refer to Steps 7–8 for Basic Canes 1 on page 28. Roll the blend into a pinroll. If a lighter color is desired on the inside of the roll, begin rolling there.

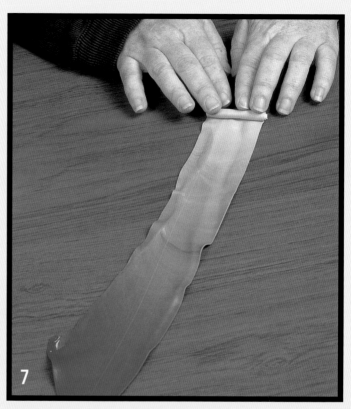

8. Roll a #5 sheet from the outside color. Wrap the sheet around the cane to maximize the effect of the blend.

9. Repeat Steps 1–8 for the green and white clays.

"Thank you, Judith."

10. Refer to Reducing & Reshaping a Cane on page 21. Reduce the canes to ½". Cut the canes right in the middle and reduce one piece of each cane to a smaller size.

11. Roll a #1 sheet from remaining white clay. Roll a #3 sheet from this sheet of clay.

12. Place the brass light switch cover as a template face down on the clay. Trim the hole for the switch. Trim the clay around the brass light switch cover, leaving ¼" selvage.

14. Turn the cover so it is right side up. Using the needle tool, place the screw holes. Make an offset for the screw head to fit.

15. Cut thin slices from the canes. Press the slices onto the white clay. Note: From a distance, the effect will look like bubbles. This effect is great for the bathroom or spa switch.

16. Refer to Baking the Clay on page 19. Bake the light switch cover. Allow to cool.

13. Fold the selvages over the light switch cover and trim off excess clay.

17. Pop the clay off the brass cover. Note: Sculpey Premo is strong enough to endure without breakage—even in the boys' room.

Troubleshooting:

If the clay forms a bubble between the brass cover and the clay, eliminate it by putting the brass cover with the baked clay back into the oven and warming it. Remove the assembly while it is still warm and place it face down on a flat, heat-proof surface with a large heavy book on it until it cools.

Design Tips:

Double-up the triangles of color to get more gradated clay for larger canes.

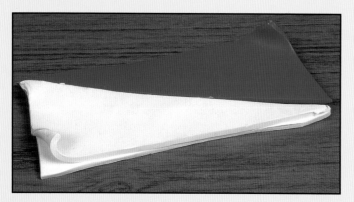

Use more than two colored triangles to create wonderful multicolored, air-brushed effects. Make the triangles in the shape below to use more than two colors. Marie Segal excels at this, creating spectacular effects in minutes.

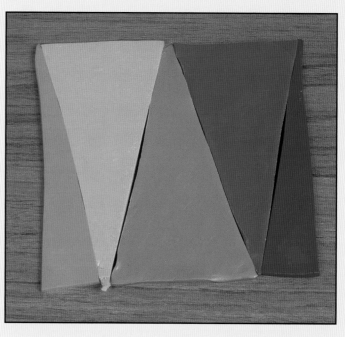

Try various color combinations, using the Skinner technique.

How do I make 3-D chain-linked canes?

Several years ago, I took a class with Pier Volkos where she showed us her lantern bead technique. I have always loved the dimensionality of that technique, so I played with it and came up with a linked effect that is spectacular in blended colors.

What You Need to Get Started:

Basic clay tools
Basic jewelry findings
Necklace clasp
Needle tool: long, thin
Sculpey Premo clay in 2 oz. packages: pearl blue (2); ecru (2); pearl green (2)
Stringing material

3-D Chain-linked Necklace

Here's How:

1. Refer to Steps 1–8 for Basic Canes 1 on page 28. Make a pinroll cane from ¾ package each of blue and ecru clays. Refer to Reducing & Reshaping a Cane on page 21. Reduce the cane to ½" diameter.

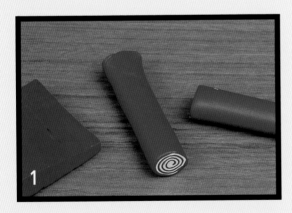

3. Refer to Steps 1–6 for Basic Canes 11 on page 51. Blend a little ecru clay into the blue clay. Make a pinroll cane from this blend and ecru clay. Allow all canes to rest 30 minutes.

2. Make a pinroll cane from ¾ package each of green and ecru clays. Reduce the cane to ½" diameter.

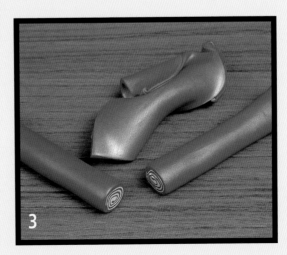

4. Cut two ³⁄₁₆"-thick slices from the blue cane. Place these two slices right next to each other so that they touch.

5. Cut a ³⁄₁₆"-thick slice from the green cane. Cut this slice in half and place the two pieces so that each half bridges the two blue slices from center to center, creating a linked bead.

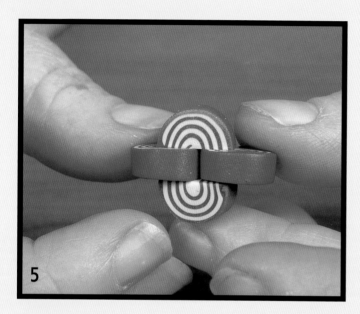

6. Repeat Steps 1–5 with the other colors to create a couple of beads from each.

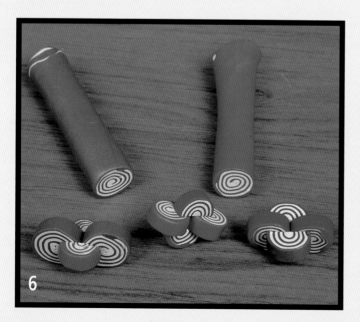

7. Using the needle tool, pierce each bead by twisting it, halfway through the length of the bead. Complete the pierce from the other side of the bead.

8. To make a couple of single lantern beads (Pier Volkos style), cut two slices in half and attach the four halves to a cylinder of color.

9. Using the needle tool, pierce each bead by twisting it, halfway through the central cylinder of the bead. Complete the pierce from the other side of the bead.

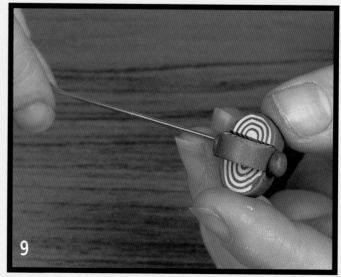

10. Cut slices from the remaining pinroll canes for additional beads. Reduce some of these canes to create smaller beads for placement at the top of the necklace.

11. Refer to Baking the Clay on page 19. Bake the beads. Allow to cool.

12. Refer to Steps 21–22 for Basic Canes 4 on page 34. Place the beads onto stringing material to length desired and attach necklace clasp to create a necklace.

Design Tips:

The same type bead can be made with blended canes, unblended canes and checkerboard cane, and whatever combinations you can think of.

The links hold up quite well if the canes are fresh when you put them together and then allow them to sit overnight before baking. I imagine this allows the separate pieces of polymer to bond together better. I have had to repair a only few of my linked beads with super strength craft adhesive.

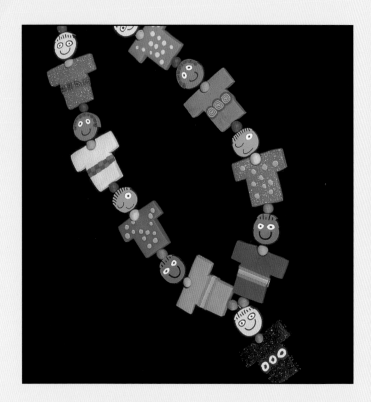

Section 3: *pictorial canes*

1
pictorial

How do I make a simple flower cane?

This pattern is perfect for drawer pulls or buttons. Kids love this pattern. I would like to try making it from Sculpey III Glow-In-the-Dark colors with a black background—one of those days when I have nothing but time! Sigh, I'll put it on the list.

What You Need to Get Started:

Basic clay tools
Drawer pulls:
  round, ceramic
  or wooden
Sculpey Premo
  clay in 2 oz.
  packages:
  cobalt blue (2);
  green (1);
  orange (1);
  cad yellow (2)

Flower Drawer Pulls

Here's How:
1. Refer to Steps 1–3 for Basic Canes 5 on page 38. Roll a cylinder from ½ package of yellow clay. Roll a #1 sheet from green clay. Wrap the sheet of green clay around the cylinder to make a bull's eye cane.

2. Refer to Reducing & Reshaping a Cane on page 21. Reduce the cane.

3. Cut the cane into five equal pieces. Assemble the pieces.

4. Repeat Steps 2–3.

5. Reduce this cane to ½" diameter and set aside. Note: You have now made a lace cane.

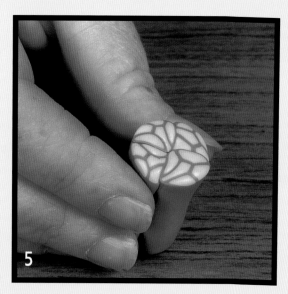

6. Refer to Steps 1–7 for Basic Canes 11 on page 51. Make a blended cane from ¾ package each of orange and yellow clays to create a blend from orange and yellow. Begin rolling at the yellow end of the sheet.

7. Wrap this cane with a #5 sheet made from the remaining orange clay.

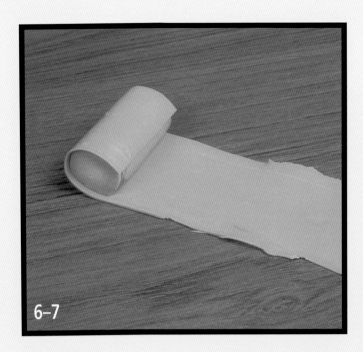

Note: We are assembling the cane vertically now, instead of horizontally.

8. Reduce this cane to ¼" diameter.

9. Cut the cane into five equal pieces. Stand these five pieces up so that they touch each other, creating the "petals."

11. Roll a snake from ½ package of blue clay. Reshape the snake to form a triangle. Cut the triangle into five equal pieces.

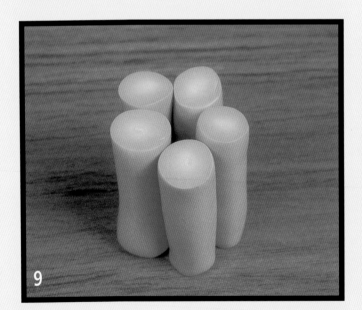

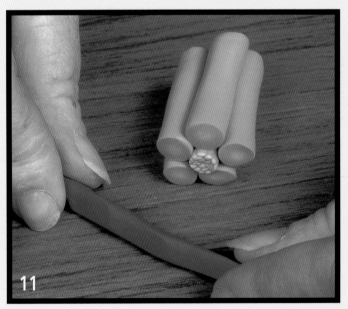

10. Determine the center of the five petals and adjust the lace cane to fit into this space. Place the lace cane into the center of the petals.

12. Place a triangle of blue between each petal. Note: The triangle should be wider at the base of the triangle and about as deep as the space of the petal.

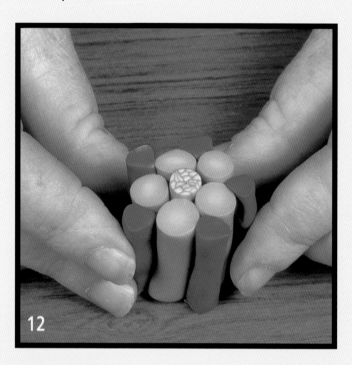

13. Wrap a #1 sheet of blue clay around the outside of this clay assemblage.

14. Reduce the cane down to 1" diameter. Note: The diameter of the cane depends on the size and condition of the drawer pull.

15. Cover the entire drawer pull with a #1 sheet of blue clay.

16. Cut a ⅛"-thick slice from the cane. Center the cane slice on the top of the covered drawer pull.

17. Gently roll the drawer pull in your hands, blending the cane slice into the covered drawer pull.

18. Refer to Baking the Clay on page 19. Bake the covered drawer pulls. Allow to cool.

How do I make a millefiori bead?

Millefiori is the famous Italian technique for lampworked glass beads. The glass artist touches a rod of glass containing a flower pattern to a molten bead, leaving a small part of the rod attached to the new bead. This is where the canework concept comes from.

What You Need to Get Started:

Backpack clip kit with header pin
Basic clay tools
Premade flower cane
Round-nosed pliers
Sculpey Premo clay in 2 oz. package: color of the cane or a complementary color

Backpack Clip

Here's How:

1. Refer to Reducing & Reshaping a Cane on page 21. Reduce the premade cane to ¼" diameter.

2. Roll a 1"-diameter ball from selected color of clay.

3. Cut thin slices from the flower cane.

4. Place the slices in a random fashion, completely covering the ball.

5. Cup your hands and slowly roll the cane-covered ball, blending the cane slices into the original ball. Frequently reverse the direction of the roll.

6. Using the needle tool, pierce the ball by twisting it halfway through. Complete the pierce from the other side of the ball.

7. Refer to Baking the Clay on page 19. Bake the ball. Allow to cool.

8. Place the ball on the header pin.

9. Using the pliers, trim the pin to ¼" longer than ball.

10. Grip the top of the pin. Roll the pliers to form a circle.

11. Thread the backpack clip on and close the loop.

3
pictorial

What You Need to Get Started:

Basic clay tools
Pin back: 1"
Sculpey Premo
  clay in 2 oz.
  packages:
  cobalt blue (2);
  ultramarine
  blue (1); cad
  yellow (2);
  zinc yellow (1)

Z Kripke says, "You can never have too much star cane." Star shapes are prevalent throughout the history of art, so she must be right.

Lapel Pin

Here's How to Make a Basic Star:

1. Refer to Steps 1–3 for Basic Canes 5 on page 38. Roll a cylinder from one package of cad yellow clay. Roll a #1 sheet from zinc yellow clay. Wrap the sheet of zinc yellow clay around the cylinder to make a bull's eye cane.

2. Refer to Reducing & Reshaping a Cane on page 21. Reshape the bull's eye cane to form a triangle.

3. Reduce the triangle cane so each side is ¼" wide.

4. Cut the triangle cane into five equal pieces.

5. Stand the pieces on end in a circle so that the bottom two points touch and the other point is facing out.

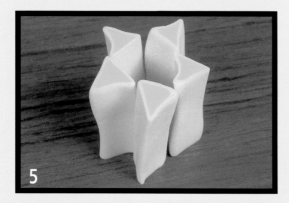

6. Roll a cylinder from cad yellow clay.

7. Determine the center of the five triangles and adjust the cylinder to fit into this space. Place the cylinder into the center of the triangles. Set this formation aside.

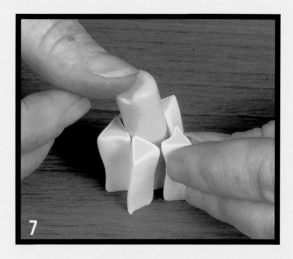

8. Roll a 1"-diameter ball from blue clay. Flatten the clay ball to a cylinder.

9. Reshape the cylinder to form a triangle.

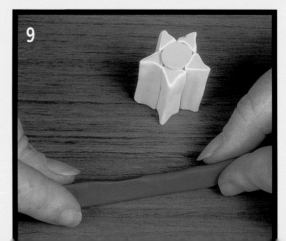

10. Reduce the triangle cane so each side is ¼" wide.

11. Cut the triangle into 10 equal pieces and fit two pieces between each arm of the star.

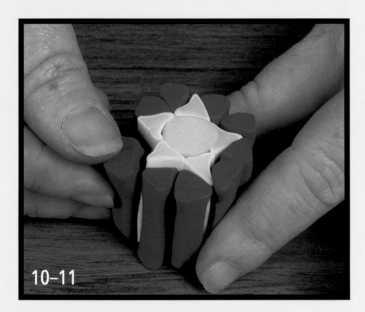

10–11

12. Roll a #1 sheet from blue clay. Wrap the sheet of blue clay around the assemblage to "pad" the pointed arms.

12

13. Reduce the entire cane to ⅜" diameter.

13

14. Cut the cane right in the middle. Set aside.

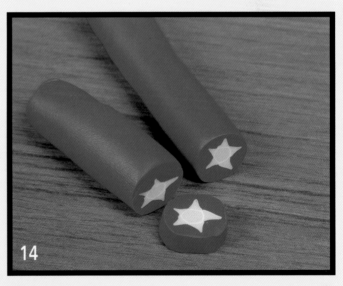

14

15. Roll a #1 sheet from ¼ package of cad yellow clay.

16. Place a 2"-diameter round form on the sheet. Cut the clay around the form.

17. Reposition the form on the clay so that a crescent shape is formed. Cut it out. Note: The sharper the edge of the form, the easier it is to trace around it.

18. Cut ⅛"-thick slices from the star cane. Apply the slices on top of and leading away from the crescent. Note: Back the projecting pieces with a #4 sheet of blue clay attached to the crescent to support the design if it gets really freeform away from the crescent.

19. Refer to Baking the Clay on page 19. Bake the assemblage. Allow to cool.

20. Place the pin back onto the back of the crescent. Attach the pin back by placing a small piece of clay over the flat part of the pin back, creating a "bandage." Rebake the clay. Allow to cool.

Design Tip:
No one says the star has to be a solid color. Try making it with blended canes, patterned canes or leftover canes in the center portion.

How do I make a face cane?

I found some face drawings in my five-year-old son's backpack and they were exactly what I was looking for—bold, simple, funky, and easy. We decided to make the faces different colors and vary their expressions and hair. Koji (my son) suggested that I combine them with little polymer shirts we cut out and they became my infamous kid necklaces.

Barrette or barrette finding: suitable for oven temperatures
Basic clay tools
Craft adhesive: super strength
Sculpey Premo clay in 2 oz. packages: black (2); ecru (2); fuchsia (1); red (1); violet (2); white (2); yellow (2)

Barrette

Here's How to Make the Ecru Boy:

1. Roll a small snake from black clay.

2. Roll two sheets from white clay. One at a time, wrap the sheets around the black snake.

3. Roll a #4 sheet from black clay. Wrap the sheet around the black and white clay combination.

4. Refer to Reducing & Reshaping a Cane on page 21. Reduce the cane to ¼" diameter or slightly smaller.

5. Cut two 2"-long pieces from the cane for the eyes.

6. Roll a #1 and a #3 sheet from ecru clay. Wrap the #1 and then the #3 sheet of ecru clay around each piece of eye cane.

7. Stand the two canes up. Cut a slice off part of the #3 sheet at the seam. Note: This cut is what keeps the eyes round when reducing the cane.

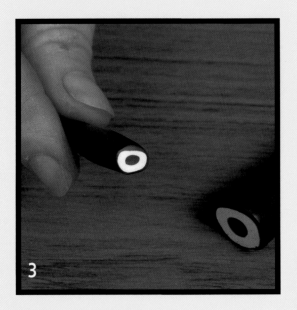

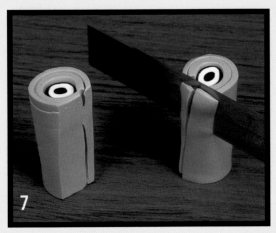

8. Roll a cylinder from ecru clay. Reshape the cylinder to form a triangle. Cut two pieces from the triangle and place these pieces between the eye canes at the top and bottom. Notice that the shape is a rectangle again.

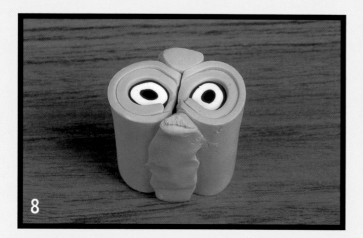

9. Roll a ⅜"-diameter cylinder from ecru clay.

10. Trim this cylinder to the length of the eye cane and cut it in half lengthwise.

11. Roll a #5 sheet from black clay. Wrap the sheet around one of the ecru halves, taking care not to cover the flat portion and creating a mouth piece.

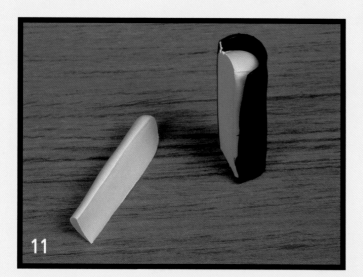

12. Attach the mouth by centering it under the eyes and slightly pressing the assemblage together.

13. Place two triangles of ecru on either side of the mouth to bring the assemblage back to a round shape. Note: Always try to bring the assemblages back to the shape into which you plan to reduce the cane.

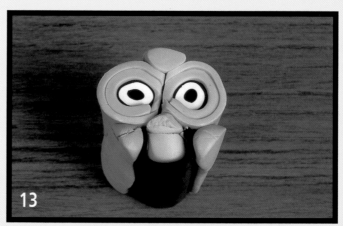

14. Roll a #1 sheet from ecru clay. Wrap the sheet around the bottom half of the assemblage from cheek to cheek.

15. Roll a #5 sheet from black clay. Roll a #4 sheet from ecru clay. Create the crewcuts by stacking the sheets. Cut the stacked layers to different heights and assemble them together on the top of the head. Note: Make certain to vary the height of the layers for tousled hair.

15

16. Roll a #5 sheet from black clay. Wrap the black sheet from one side of the hairline, under the face, to the other.

16

17. Reduce the cane to diameter desired. Cut slices as desired.

17

Here's How to Make the Purple Girl:

Note: The little purple girl has Skinner blended cheeks added to her assemblage. She is decked in curls on top.

1. Refer to Steps 1–12 for Here's How to Make the Ecru Boy on page 67. Assemble the face cane substituting violet clay for ecru clay.

2. Refer to Steps 1–7 for Basic Canes 11 on page 51. Make a blended cane from fuchsia clay and white clay proportionate to the size of the face cane.

3. Roll a small cylinder from the violet clay. Reshape the cylinder to form a triangle. Tuck the triangle into the area formed by the mouth and the eyes.

3

4. Set the blended canes into the assemblage for cheeks. Complete the shape with a couple more small triangles of violet clay.

4

5. Refer to Basic Canes 1 on page 28. Make a pinroll cane from violet clay rolled with black clay for the hair.

6. Refer to Reducing & Reshaping a Cane on page 21. Reduce the pinroll cane and cut it into several pieces.

7. Add the pieces of the pinroll cane to the top of the face for curly hair.

8. Roll a #1 and a #5 sheet from black clay. Wrap the #1 sheet over the hair. Wrap the #5 sheet from one side of the hairline, under the face, to the other.

9. Reduce the cane to diameter desired. Cut slices as desired.

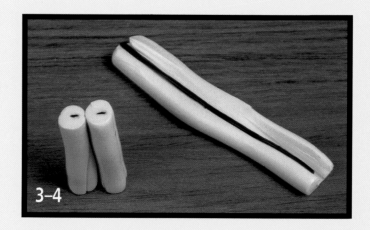

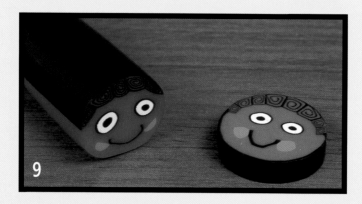

Here's How to Make the Boy with Tongue:
1. Mix yellow and white clays 3:1. Roll a ½"-diameter cylinder from this mix for the eye cane.

2. Cut the cylinder in half lengthwise.

3. Roll a #5 sheet from black clay. Cut and insert a small strip from the sheet between the two halves of the cylinder and center it within the cylinder.

4. Gently press the cylinder back together and roll it on the work surface to the size desired to begin construction.

5. Refer to Steps 7–8 for Here's How to Make the Ecru Boy on page 67. Begin assembling the face, substituting yellow clay mix for ecru clay.

6. Roll a cylinder of red clay the same size as one of the eyes.

7. Trim the cylinder to the same height as the face assemblage.

8. Make a cut lengthwise down the center of the cylinder. This cut should be just one third of the way through.

9. Insert the straight edge of a #5 sheet of black clay into this cut and trim it flush with the cylinder.

10. Gently press the cylinder back together and roll it on the work surface, without reducing it.

11. Stand the cylinder up. Cut a slice off part of the cylinder to give it a flattened edge. The black insert should be roughly centered in the flat edge now.

12. Wrap the bottom rounded portion of the cylinder with a #5 sheet of black clay.

13. Roll a #3 sheet from black clay. Cut and place a portion of the sheet to cover and extend beyond the flattened edge of the cylinder.

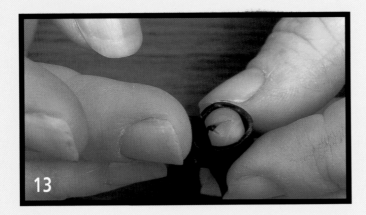

14. Roll a #3 or #4 sheet from yellow clay mix. Wrap the sheet around the tongue to even out the black, "padding" the tongue and supporting that upper lip of black clay .

15. Refer to Steps 13–17 for Here's How to Make the Ecru Boy on page 67, substituting the yellow clay mix for ecru clay. Add the tongue assemblage to the face assemblage and complete the face cane.

Here's How to Make the Orange Boy:
1. Mix orange and white clays 3:1.

2. Refer to Steps 1–17 for Here's How to Make the Ecru Boy on page 67. Assemble the face cane substituting orange clay mix for ecru clay.

Here's How to Make the Barrett:
1. Roll two #1 sheets from the black clay. Stack the sheets for the base. Trim as desired.

2. Cut slices from the face canes and arrange them on the base. Decorate the exposed base with small dots of colored clay.

3. Refer to Baking the Clay on page 19. Bake the clay right on the surface of the barrette. Allow to cool.

4. Pop the clay off the barrette. Using craft adhesive, adhere it back onto the barrette for more durability.

5
pictorial

How do I make a snowman cane?

For my annual holiday pin, I made a great little pin using my basic face and a piece of an old flower cane reduced quite small.

What You Need to Get Started:

Basic clay tools
Craft adhesive:
  super strength
Pin back
Premade flower
  cane
Sculpey Premo
  clay in 2 oz.
  packages: black
  (2); white (4)
SuperFlex clay:
  orange (1)

Snowman Pin

Here's How:
1. Refer to Steps 1–14 for How to Make the Ecru Boy on page 67. Assemble the face, substituting white for ecru clay.

2. Roll a #1 sheet from black clay. Wrap the sheet around the assemblage.

3. Refer to Reducing & Reshaping a Cane on page 21. Reduce the cane to ⅝" diameter.

4. Cut a 3"-long piece from the cane. Set aside.

5. Roll a cylinder from two packages of white clay.

6. Cut this cylinder right in the middle. Reduce one piece to ⅝" diameter and the other piece to ¾" diameter. These cylinders should be as long as the face cane.

7. Roll two #4 sheets from black clay. Wrap one sheet around each cylinder.

8. Stack the face cylinder on top of the smaller all-white cylinder. Stack these two on top of the larger all-white cylinder. Lightly press these cylinders together, taking care not to distort the cylinders too much.

9. For the top of the hat, make a rectangle with the remaining black clay that is as long as the three cylinders.

10. For the brim of the hat, place the rectangle on a #1 strip of black clay.

11. Place the hat assemblage on top of the snowman and press it into place. Allow the whole assemblage to rest 20 minutes.

12. Cut slices from the snowman cane, from the top of the hat to the bottom of the snowman.

13. For the carrot nose, roll ⅓ package of the orange clay into a snake and reduce one end to a small point. Cut this point off. Remake the point and cut it off for each snowman.

14. Using the back of the blade, make rings around the carrot for texture.

15. Using a tiny bit of super strength craft adhesive, adhere the carrot onto the face.

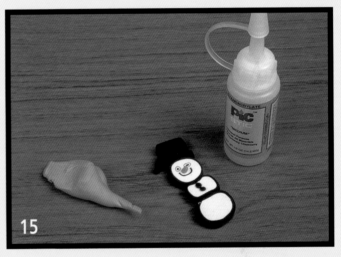

16. Cut a thin slice from the flower cane. Using the blade, separate the petals a little. Gently press the flower onto the hat for decoration.

17. Press tiny bits of black clay onto the snow-man's body for "coal."

18. Refer to Baking the Clay on page 19. Bake the snowman. Allow to cool.

19. Using super strength craft adhesive, adhere the pin back onto the back of the snowman.

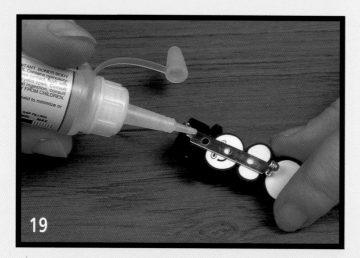

Troubleshooting:

Use a new blade on the cutting tool to help keep the snowman from flattening too much when you cut it.

Remember that the nose is glued on. You can bake the glue, but you should check for brittleness after it has baked and cooled. Sometimes you will need to reglue the nose after baking.

Design Tips:

Refer to Step 20 for Pictorial 3 on page 66. Finish this pin more professionally by applying a bandage of clay to the pin back.

These pins make great gifts. Make your own personalized gift tags with the snowman glued to the side of the tag. Mine lives on one of my hats, along with his snowman buddy, made by Janie Wolfe.

How do I make a shaman cane?

This cane has launched many a clay addiction, including my own. My first attempt was successful, thanks to Z Kripke. But what is really important is that this cane gave me the skills to produce other pictorial canes, including a Kokopelli that I made the next day. It was a baby step, but I had taken the technique and moved it one step further.

What You Need to Get Started:

Basic clay tools
Drafting vellum
   or baking
   parchment
Sculpey Premo
   clay in 2 oz.
   packages: black
   (3); ecru (4);
   turquoise (1)

Postcard

Here's How:

1. Refer to Steps 1–8 for Basic Canes 10 on page 48. Make a small checkerboard cane from black and ecru clays.

2. Refer to Reducing & Reshaping a Cane on page 21. Reduce the checkerboard cane to ¾".

3. Cut a 1½"-long piece from the cane.

4. Roll a #5 sheet from black clay. Wrap the sheet around the cane.

5. Roll a #4 sheet from turquoise clay. Place the sheet on one side of the checkerboard.

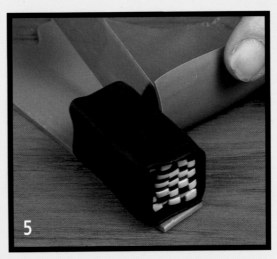

6. Roll a #3 sheet from turquoise clay and a #3 sheet from black clay. Trim each sheet to the width of the cane as if adding them as a wrap.

7. Stack the two sheets of clay together and cut into ⅛"-thick matchsticks. These matchsticks will become the "fringe" on the "robe."

8. Attach the fringe to the checker-board to form the robe by placing the matchsticks along the edge of the cane, alternating the colors of the layered squares. Gently squeeze the matchsticks into place as there is usually some gaping on the outside edges.

9. For the head, roll a cylinder from black clay that is proportionate to the robe.

10. Roll two #1 sheets from ecru clay. One at a time, wrap the sheets around the black cylinder. Roll a #3 sheet from black clay. Cut this sheet to the same size as the ecru wraps.

11. Cut through the ecru wraps and insert a piece from the sheet of black clay. Trim this area flat to fit on top of the robe.

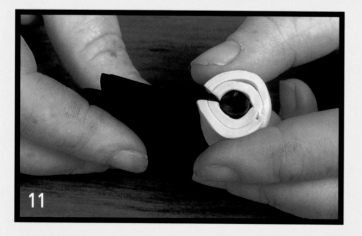

12. Place the head assemblage on top of the robe assemblage.

13. For the arms, roll a #1 sheet from black clay. Trim the sheet to 1½" (the depth of the assemblage). Cut this sheet in half lengthwise.

14. Place one arm at each side of the top of the robe and wrap them up and around the head assemblage. Trim the arms to create a ¼" gap where they meet at the top.

Note: This is the trick to adding lines to canes. Remember that they have to go all the way through the cane, so it is not just a line on top, but a layer throughout.

15. Roll a #1 sheet from turquoise clay. Cut a small piece from the sheet and place it in the gap created by the black arms. Note: This will simulate a turquoise plate.

16. For the legs, roll a #1 sheet from black clay. Cut this sheet in half lengthwise and to proportionate lengths for legs. Place each piece at the bottom of the robe. Set remaining pieces aside.

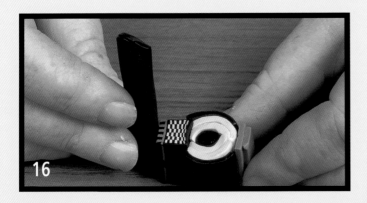

16

21. Fill in all other places in the assemblage with ecru clay to bring the entire piece to a rectangle. Note: Place triangles of ecru clay to delineate a corner. Sometimes, wrapping a #1 sheet of the ecru clay around the central image will prevent "chopping" in the outside lines of the image by too many pieces of background material.

17. Make a rectangle from ecru clay to fit between the legs and to support them.

17

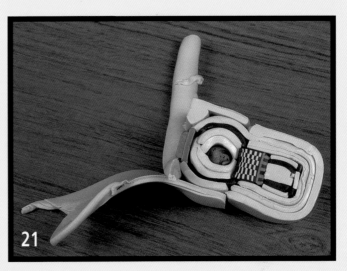

21

18. Make and place rectangles of ecru on the outside of the legs, even with the edges of the robe.

19. For the feet, cut strips from remaining pieces of the #1 sheet of black clay. Add these feet pieces at the bottom of the legs.

22. Roll at least two #1 sheets from the ecru clay. One at a time, wrap the sheets around the bottom of the cane to prevent distortion.

20. Finish the layer with a small piece cut from the #1 sheet of ecru to even out the assemblage.

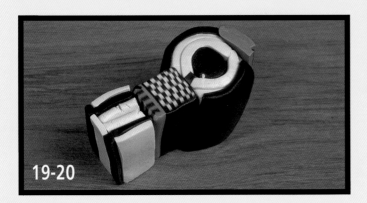

19-20

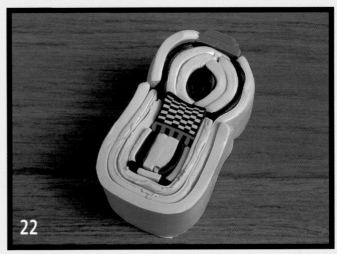

22

23. Reduce the cane to the size desired.

24. For the postcard, roll a #1 and a #4 sheet from the ecru clay, each measuring 3" x 5" and sandwich them together. Cut them into an irregular shape.

25. Refer to Basic Canes 1 on page 28. Create some small pinroll canes from scrap clay.

26. Cut thin slices from the Shaman cane and the pinroll canes. Randomly place the slices on the postcard.

27. Place the parchment or vellum over the piece. Rub gently to press the cane slices into the ecru clay. Note: The paper helps to seal the edges of the clays and remove the seams. Do not press too much or the piece will become too thin.

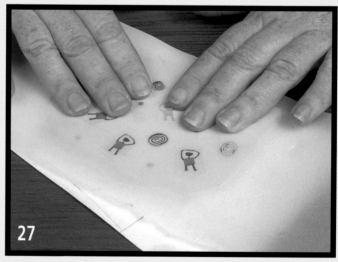

28. Using the rock, lightly texture the entire piece. Note: My round rock is one of my closely guarded treasures from my boys. I can just roll it across the surface for even texturing.

28

29. Refer to Baking the Clay on page 19. Bake the postcard. Allow to cool.

30. Write the greeting and address on the back of the postcard. Note: Make certain to take the postcard to the post office for hand canceling.

Design Tips:
Make the robe in any pattern you would like and reduce it to the size you wish to start the cane.

Change what the Shaman is holding—add a star; add a heart.

Change the entire cane by adding wraps to the outside, matchstick checkerboards, etc.

Note: These cane slices are from my collection made by Z Kripke, Maddux, and me.

How do I make a heart-shaped cane?

What You Need to Get Started:

Basic clay tools
Needle tool: long, thin
Premade pinroll canes
Sculpey Premo clay in 2 oz. package: coordinating color (1)
T-pin and French loop wire for earring assembly

I used a heart-shaped cane for the item a Shaman held up one year for Valentines Day. I didn't know it at the time that hearts are supposedly one of the most difficult shapes to cane! Sometimes ignorance is bliss.

Heart Earrings

Here's How to Make a Pinroll Heart:
1. Refer to Reducing & Reshaping a Cane on page 21. Reduce the pinroll cane to ½" diameter.

2. Cut two 1"–3" long pieces from cane, depending on the amount of cane available and how many hearts you wish to produce.

3. Place the two pieces of cane side-by-side and lightly press them together.

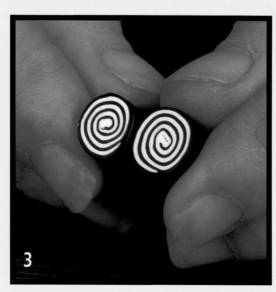

4. Pull the bottoms of the two canes together in a point with your fingers. You will need to work your fingers down the cane to do this. After the point is achieved, slide your fingers down the cane to smooth out the pointed shape.

5. If the top of the heart got too pressed together, set the back of the blade in the middle of the canes and lean it out to each side to re-accent the two parts of the heart. Allow the cane to rest.

6. Cut thin slices from the cane.

7. Make small beads by rolling a snake from coordinating colored clay first and cutting it into equal-sized pieces. Roll each piece into a bead.

8. Using the needle tool, pierce each bead by twisting it halfway through the bead. Complete the pierce from the other side of the bead, resealing the points as they are pierced.

9. Refer to Steps 7–11 for Basic Canes 2 on page 30. Place beads on earring findings.

Section 4: *molds & textural effects*

1
effects

What You Need to Get Started:

Baby powder
Basic clay tools
Brass light switch cover
Clay mold: leaf
Granitex clay: black (1); blue (2); green (1)
Needle tool: large

Clay molds produce a variety of fast and easy clay shapes that can be used as individual pieces of art or to embellish a larger project. This decorative light switch cover and the leaves that are on it are made from a premade stone-effect clay called Granitex. The light switch cover appears to have been sculpted from colored granite.

Leaf Light Switch Cover

Here's How:
1. Roll a #3 sheet from the blue clay and place it on the work surface.

2. Place the brass light switch cover as a template face down on the clay. Trim the hole for the switch. Trim the clay around the brass light switch cover, leaving ¼" selvage.

3. Fold the selvages over the light switch cover and trim off excess clay.

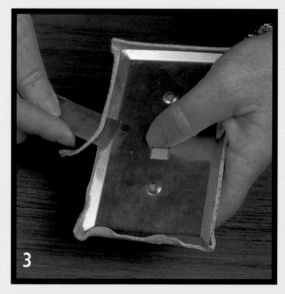

4. Turn the cover so it is right side up. Using the needle tool, place the screw holes. Make an offset for the screw head to fit.

5. Roll the green clay into a slightly pointed ball. Dust the clay ball or the mold with baby powder. Press the clay

ball into the leaf mold. Slice across the surface of the mold to remove the excess clay.

8. Refer to Baking the Clay on page 19. Bake the light switch cover. Allow to cool.

9. Pop the clay off the brass cover.

Design Tip:
For autumn leaves, try blending small amounts of gold, orange, and red clays into the green Granitex.

6. Remove clay from the mold by lightly pressing the excess clay onto the back of the clay still in the mold. The clay in the mold should stick to the excess enough to lift it out of the mold.

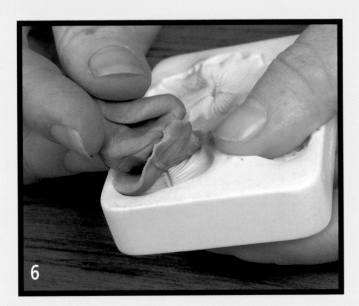

7. Place the leaves onto the blue clay and press to make surface contact.

How do I use household objects to make a reverse impression?

What You Need to Get Started:

Acrylic paint: brown
Baby powder
Basic clay tools
Brass light switch cover
Brush: small
Cotton cloth
Needle tool: large
Plastic dinosaurs or plastic ferns: small
Rock for texturing
Sculpey Premo clay in 2 oz. packages: ecru (2)

As I mentioned before, don't overlook household objects, such as those found in your children's toy boxes as resources for wonderful textures and molds. I once had a student bring an antique Chinese chop, or signature stamp, to class. The image was of a carp, we made a reverse mold of the image and created some wonderful pieces with it.

Fossils Light Switch Cover

Here's How:
1. Roll a #3 sheet from the ecru clay and place it on the work surface.

2. Place the brass light switch cover as a template face down on the sheet. Trim the hole for the switch. Trim the clay around the brass light switch cover, leaving ¼" selvage.

3. Fold the selvages over the light switch cover and trim off excess clay.

4. Turn the cover so it is right side up. Using the needle tool, place the screw holes. Make an offset for the screw head to fit.

5. Using the rock, texture the entire surface of the clay. If desired, add a small amount of organic material such as dirt to the surface of the clay as you texture. Note: My round rock is perfect for this procedure. Since it is sandstone, it actually embeds sand into the clay as I use it.

5a

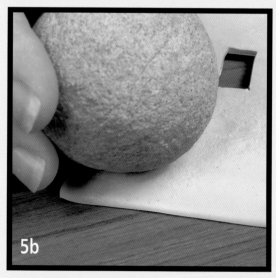

5b

6. Dust the dinosaurs or ferns with baby powder and press them into the surface of the clay. Roll them slightly to get a full impression.

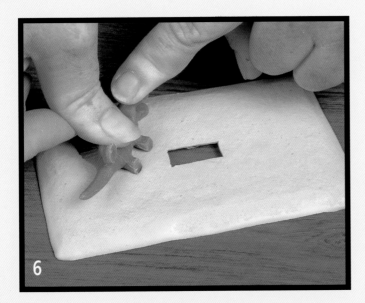

7. Refer to Baking the Clay on page 19. Bake the light switch cover. Allow to cool.

8. Pop the clay off the brass cover.

9. Mix the paint with a little water and wash the surface of the baked clay, allowing the paint to pool in the depressions.

10. Using the cotton cloth, lightly wipe the surface.

11. Repeat Steps 9–10 until you are pleased with the effect.

Troubleshooting:

Watch out for small text written on the dinosaurs. It won't show up until they are baked and antiqued. I don't think you would really find "Made in China" in any prehistoric wall art.

Design Tips:

Experiment with this technique by making or covering pendants, pens, magnets, etc.

Look for molding possibilities in unexpected places. Once, I went looking in the bathtub. Low and behold, there was a perfect little plastic fish. I did some modification on it and made a mold. The result was pretty satisfying.

3
effects

What You Need to Get Started:

Acrylic paint:
   brown
Baby powder
Basic clay tools
Box, round:
   cardboard,
   metal, or
   wooden
Brush
Cotton cloth
Craft adhesive:
   all purpose
Sculpey III or
   Super Sculpey:
   scraps
Sculpey Premo
   clay in 2 oz.
   packages: ecru
   (3)
Shells: several
   different shapes
   and sizes

How do I make a mold?

I live at the beach and finding interesting shells to use for molds is a part-time summer job for my boys. Don't overlook barnacles and interesting rocks either.

Seashell Box

Here's How:

1. If using a wooden or cardboard box, prepare the surface by painting a layer of all purpose craft adhesive on it and allowing it to dry. This will help the clay to adhere to the nonporous surface.

2. Prepare the molds by making a flattened ball of the Sculpey III or Super Sculpey scrap clay that is about ¼" larger all around than the shell.

3. Dust the outside of the shell with baby powder and press it evenly into the clay.

4. Remove the shell by lifting up on both ends of the shell at once and pulling straight up.

5. Refer to Baking the Clay on page 19. Bake the mold. Allow to cool.

6. Roll a #3 sheet from ecru clay and place it on the work surface. Place the top of the box lid face down on the sheet of clay. Trim around the lid, leaving enough clay to cover the sides of the lid.

7. Fold the clay down around the sides of the lid and trim. You may have to overlap the clay, like wrapping a package. Press these overlaps and trim off the excess.

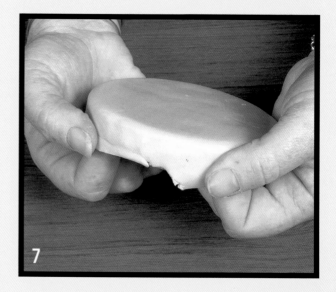

88

8. Roll another #3 sheet from ecru clay and cover the sides of the box, leaving the upper edge free of clay so the lid still fits on the box.

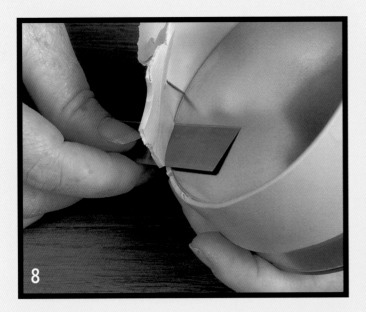

9. Roll a #4 sheet from ecru clay. Place the box on this sheet. Trim around the box to cover the bottom of the box. Smooth the edges of the bottom into the side edges of clay.

10. Using the rock, texture the clay surfaces, except the bottom. Make a couple of uneven

areas for a more natural feel. Add some "organic materials" to the surface if desired. Note: Remember that my "magic" sandstone rock leaves particles of dirt and sand behind.

11. Roll a slightly pointed ball from ecru clay and dust the surface of the point with baby powder. Press the point into the shell mold and trim off the excess clay.

12. Use the excess clay to "lift" the clay from the mold.

13. Place the clay shells on the surface of the clay-covered lid as desired. Press shells into place when satisfied with the design.

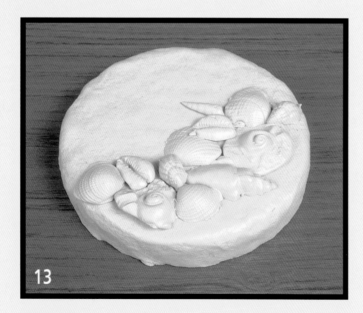

14. Using another smaller piece of rock, blend and feather the edges of the shells into the surface clay so they appear to be formed out of the rock surface.

15. Refer to Baking the Clay on page 19. Bake the box. Allow to cool.

16. Mix the paint with a little water and wash the surface of the box, allowing the paint to pool in the depressions.

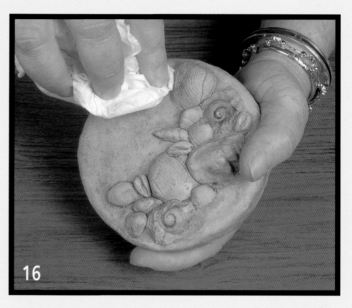

17. Lightly wipe the surface with the cotton cloth.

18. Repeat Steps 16–17 until you are pleased with the effect.

Design Tips:
Use Sculpey III or Super Sculpey for these shell molds as these clays give a rougher texture to the surface of the shells, similar to unpolished shells.

Several small shells can be molded on one larger piece of scrap clay. It is easier to find the mold among your supplies if you do this.

Cut the excess clay from the molded clay after removing it from the mold. This gives a more random edge to the mold.

I have made everything with these shells—light switch covers, necklaces, picture frames, and my favorite napkin rings.

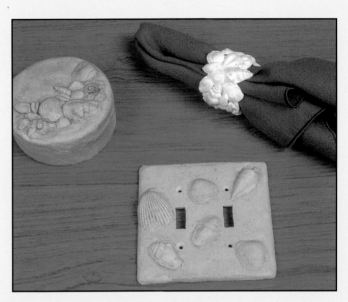

The paint tends to grab the surface more if the clay is warm. So for a heavy coat of antiquing, try treating the clay before it is completely cooled.

4
effects

How do I use colored pencils with clay?

What You Need to Get Started:

Basic clay tools
Colored pencils: soft lead
Composition metal leaf: color desired (small amount)
Cotton cloth
Round or square form
Rub-on gilt: gold
Sandpaper: fine grit
Sculpey Premo clay in 2 oz. package: pearl (1)
Varathane and brush

Colored pencils are not just for paper. They work very well with the clay medium, too. With pencils, you can quickly decorate the surface of the clay. Pearl colored clay shows through the pencil and causes the pencil to appear pearlized.

Rainbow Coasters

Here's How:
1. Roll a #1 sheet from the pearl clay large enough to accommodate the round or square form.

2. Place the form on the sheet. Cut the clay around the form. Repeat for a set.

3. Sprinkle small pieces of the composition metal leaf on the surface of the clay. Rub the metal leaf into place with your finger, blending the colors across the clay.

4. Refer to Baking the Clay on page 19. Bake the coasters. Allow to cool.

5. Using colored pencils, color the surface in any pattern desired. Color in both directions, right over the surface of the leaf, to ensure even color.

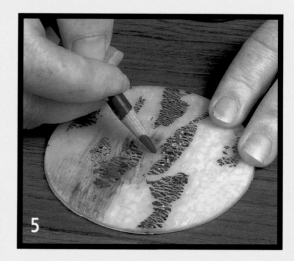

6. Using a cotton cloth, blend the colors slightly. If needed, reapply the pencil and blend again.

7. Using the fine-grit sandpaper, sand the edges of the coasters.

8. Apply rub-on gilt on the edges of the coasters.

9. Seal the surface and edges with varathane.

Design Tips:

Blend pencil colors into each other in different patterns. Try stripes, following the order of the colors in a rainbow or spots of colors over the entire coaster.

Color only a portion of the coaster, contrasting the clay and metal leaf.

How do I use
rubber stamps with clay?

Rubber stamps brushed with a translucent heat-embossing powder yield incredible textures on clay. Combined with the use of texturing tools and coordinating powders, black clay takes on the appearance of antiqued bronze. Your friends will have to look closely to see that you are not wearing a piece of ancient art.

Bracelet

Here's How:
1. Roll a #4 sheet from black clay and place it on the work surface.

2. Lightly press the bracelet blank onto the clay to get an impression of the bracelet edges.

3. Trim the clay around the impression. Press the clay into place onto the bracelet blank.

4. Using the texturing tools, randomly texture the surface of the clay, leaving some blank areas as desired.

5. Lightly rub gold translucent heat-embossing powder over the stamp. Randomly press the stamp into the textured surface of the clay.

6. Randomly layer the remaining translucent heat-embossing powders with your fingers, over-lapping the colors to create depth.

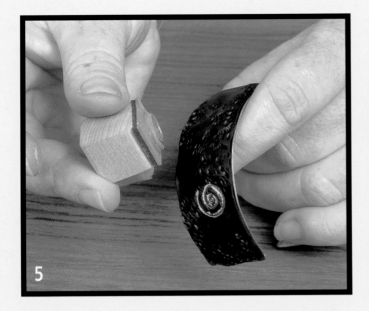

7. Refer to Baking the Clay on page 19. Bake the bracelet. Allow to cool.

8. Pop the clay off the bracelet blank. Glue it onto the surface of the blank, so the bracelet can flex for fit.

9. Using the surface sealant, seal the clay.

Design Tips:
   Apply as much or as little color as desired. Vary the color of the powder and vary the image.

   Use this combination of techniques to create anything from bracelets, to boxes, to light switch covers.

6
effects

How do I make clay look metallic?

One of my favorite variations of this technique is silver-work. I've used this combination for bracelets, boxes, pins, and even a Christmas ornament.

What You Need to Get Started:

Acrylic paint:
   black
Basic clay tools
Brush: small
Pen: round
   barrel, any
   color
Pin back
Rubber sculpting
   chisel: small
Sculpey Premo
   clay in 2 oz.
   packages: gold
   (small amount);
   silver (1)
Surface sealant
Translucent
   heat-embossing
   powders:
   antique bronze;
   super copper;
   brilliant gold

Brooch

Here's How:
1. Roll a #1 sheet from the silver clay and place it on the work surface.

2. Cut the clay to create a geometric shape. Note: This is an excellent use for kitchen sets of cutters.

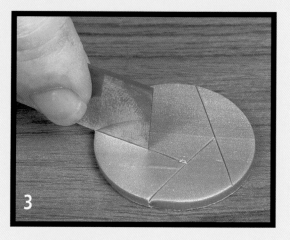

3. Using the back of the blade, draw several lines on the clay to create random geometric areas.

4. Remove the ink cartridge from the pen cylinder. Using the different parts of the pen, create designs within the geometric areas without having adjoining areas with the same pattern.

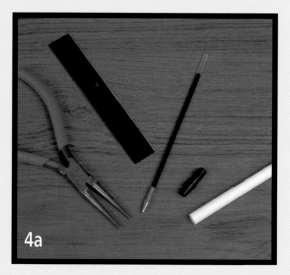

Using the point of the ink cartridge, make the small holes. Using the opposite end of the ink cartridge, form the smaller circles. Using the empty pen cylinder, form the larger circle.

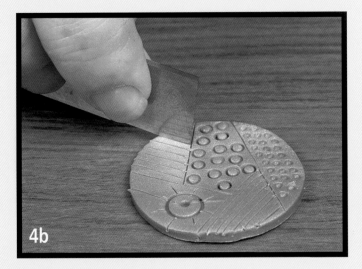

5. Once you have the textures in place, determine which areas will be which color, without having adjoining areas of the same color. Using the chisel, apply the translucent heat-embossing powders in nice even strokes. Watch the tip of the chisel to make certain you do not pick up too much powder at once. Leave some areas without powder, so that the silver shows also.

6. Refer to Step 20 for Pictorial 3 on page 66. Apply the pin back with a bandage of clay to the back of the brooch.

7. Refer to Baking the Clay on page 19. Bake the brooch. Allow to cool.

8. Mix the paint with a little water and wash the surface of the clay, allowing the paint to pool in the depressions.

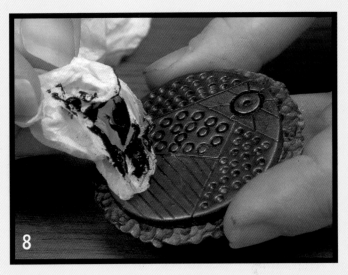

9. Lightly wipe the surface with the cotton cloth.

10. Repeat Steps 7–8 until you are pleased with the effect. Allow to dry.

11. Seal the clay with a sealant of your choice.

Design Tip:
Back the textured piece with a larger piece of textured clay. Use contrasting shapes and colors.

How do I use scrap clay?

What You Need to Get Started:

Basic clay tools
Cookie cutter:
  heart
Craft adhesive:
  super strength
Drafting vellum
  or baking
  parchment
Pin back
Premade canes:
  end pieces in
  any color and
  any pattern,
  reduced to no
  larger than ½",
  in a variety of
  diameters
Rubber sculpting
  chisel: small
Sculpey Premo
  clay: scraps
Translucent
  heat-embossing
  powder: gold

Nothing need go to waste with this medium. We have already used scrap clay inside millefiori work and as the base clay for translucent heat-embossing powders. Here are a few ways to use both scrap clay and leftover end pieces of cane.

Valentine's Day Pin

Here's How:
1. Roll a #3 sheet about 3" x 4" from scrap clay.

2. Cut very thin slices from the canes. Place the slices on the clay sheet, completely covering the surface and leaving as little space as possible between the cane slices.

4. Carefully lift the parchment or vellum to see if there are any obvious seams still showing.

3. Place the parchment or vellum over the piece. Rub gently to blend the edges of the canes together.

5. Repeat Steps 3–4 as needed.

6. Using the cookie cutter, cut a heart from this patterned clay.

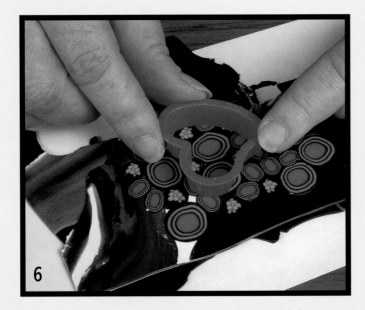

7. Using the rubber sculpting chisel, apply a little powder all along the edge of the heart if you wish to disguise the scrap clay below the canes.

8. Refer to Baking the Clay on page 19. Bake the clay heart. Allow to cool.

9. Using super strength craft adhesive, adhere the pin back onto the back of the heart.

Design Tips:
Refer to Step 20 for Pictorial 3 on page 66. Finish this pin more professionally by applying a bandage of clay to the pin back.

The finished product can be any shape you desire.

Use the same method to make an egg-shaped Easter pin, such as this one created by Julie Downing for our Gift-of-the-Month club, another innovative swap concept from Nancy Babb.

How do I make a Natasha bead?

What You Need to Get Started:

Needle tool: long
Premade canes:
  end pieces
Sculpey Premo
  clay: assorted
  scraps

This is one of the most documented and versatile techniques for using scrap clay. It is named after the woman who first described it on the world wide web. The other name for this technique is the Mirror Bead.

Natasha Bead

Here's How:
1. Roll snakes from each piece of scrap clay. Bundle the snakes and canes together.

2. Twist these bundles together tightly. The tighter you twist the finer the detail.

3. Using your fingers and an acrylic rod, form the twist into a rectangle. Cut the rectangle into smaller segments if desired.

4. Cut the rectangle in half lengthwise. Cut each of these two pieces in half lengthwise again. You now have four pieces from the original rectangle.

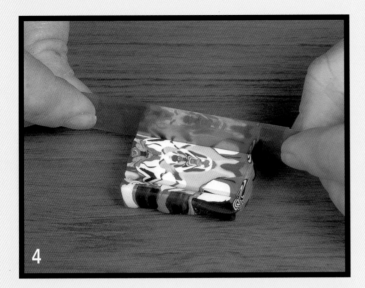

5. Rearrange the four pieces, turning them around to turn the piece inside out. Each side should be a different mirror image.

6. Using your hands and the acrylic rod, smooth the seams.

7. Trim the two ends. Top the ends with flattened balls of clay or pinch the edges together.

8. Using the needle tool, pierce each bead by twisting it halfway through the bead. Complete the pierce from the other side of the bead.

9. Refer to Baking the Clay on page 19. Bake the beads. Allow to cool.

Design Tips:
   Try using Skinner blends in this process as they are spectacular.

   Use a ripple blade to cut the four pieces and yield an entirely different effect.

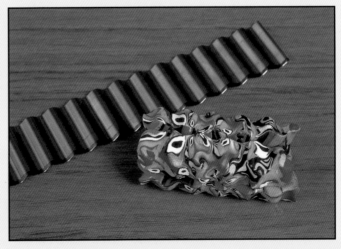

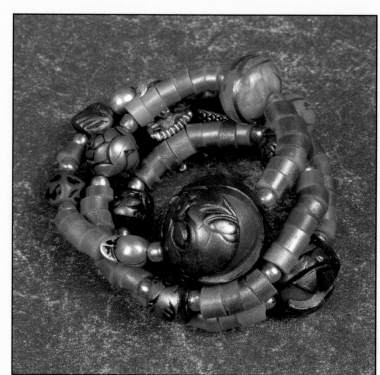

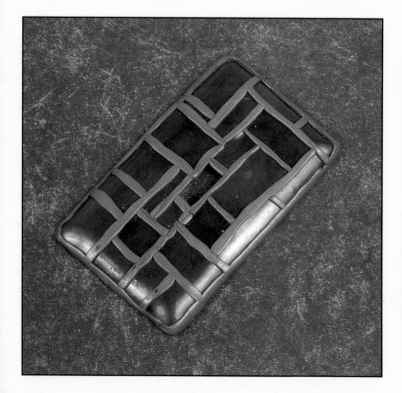

Section 5: *gallery*

Marie Segal

Wow! What vibrancy of color. Only Marie could make these little tiny odd-shaped canes with perfect detail.

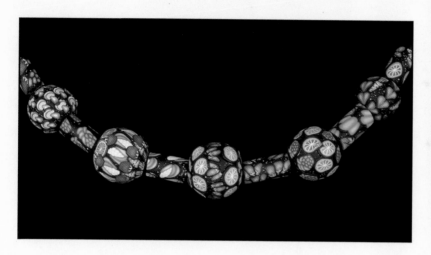

Dottie McMillan

And in her spare time she writes mystery novels... This piece is formed around a burnt-out light bulb.

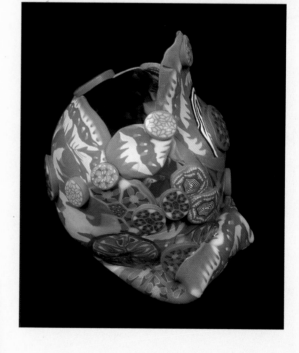

Klew

'Nuff said, she is awesome! Look at that use of color and attention to detail.

Z Kripke

You see, there is a reason we call Z Kripke our Goddess of Polymer—she was the first to show us wonderful ways with petroglyphs. I once saw this awesome woman reduce a six-month old two-pound cane by pounding it with her hands. But then again, I've seen little Marie Segal reduce 20-pound canes. There is no mercy when clay is in the hands of the Goddesses— only magic. Paleolithic man never had it so good.

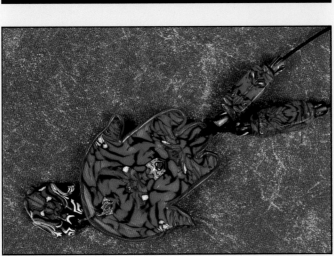

Varda Levram-Ellisman

Her work has such clean lines. Varda is the "Natasha Queen" in our Guild. Here are some of her favorite Natashas.

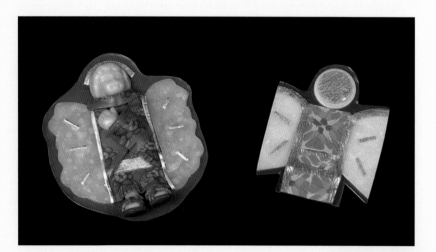

Ellie Hitchcock
Her angels should be everywhere.

Jami Miller
Her attention to detail is phenomenal. She can find more tools and gadgets and use them all to perfection.

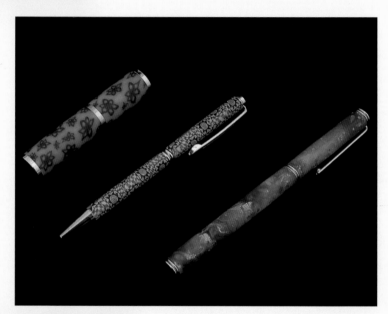

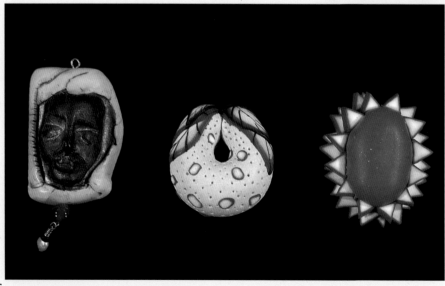

Francie Ogden
We thought we lost her talent, but she reappeared.

Karen Murphy

My most favorite piece of imitative bone. People will argue with me that it's organic.

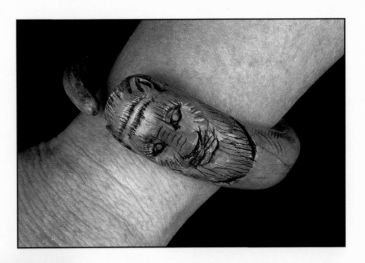

Mike Buessler

No one can cane a landscape like this man.

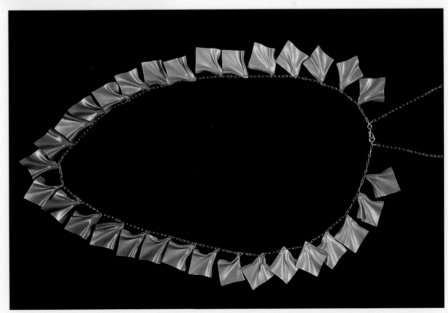

Judith Skinner

Yes, Judith is the Skinner of the Skinner Blend. Thank you Judith!

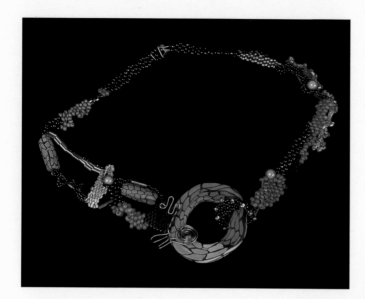

Susan Berkowitz
Multimedia at its best.

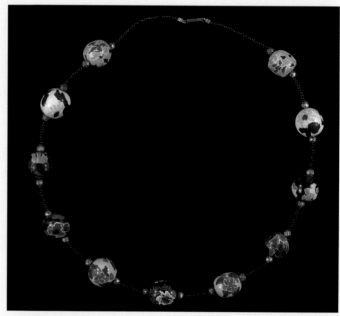

Jane Mahneke & friends

Jane's fabulous necklace is a great example of the keepsake work that can be created from trading cane slices in a polymer clay class.

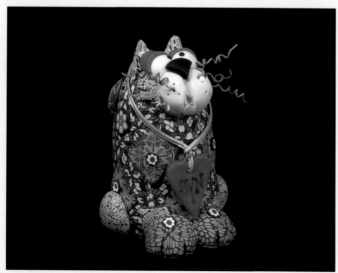

Kris Richards
Not only is Krissy a great artist, she's a great friend, too. She is one of the artists responsible for our Delphi website, Polymer Clay Central.

Jan Walcott
   Jan has discovered more polymer artists and aided more careers. AND she's talented to boot!

Yang-Yang Juan
   Her miniatures are to die for. This is my son, Tahichi.

Michalee Sloan
   I claimed Frankie before he was even finished!

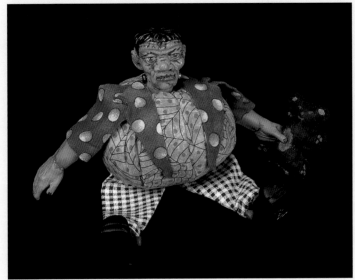

Tracy Aiello
Her work is just yummy, yes?

Shelly Comisky
Her creations are
absolutely precious.

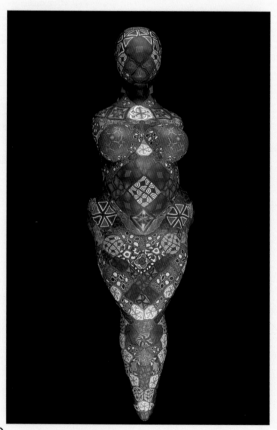

Carolyn Potter
Carolyn, one of our most treasured (and wacky)
members, suggested that we cover one of her famous
Goddess figures with cane slices made by all the Guild
members for our Guild Project this year. The colors of
purple, and earthtones were preselected and here is the
result.

Our guild creates a group sampler project like this
every year. We make two—one to raffle and one to keep
to mark our progress.

Bupleuk Geen Yo
Thomas Kum

There are over 40 hours of sanding alone invested in this piece. You should see his truck!

Tom says, "The bike was a gift from my friend Clinto Abbott. Inspiration for the artwork comes from Aone Jones. Finally, I would like to thank syn, Howard, and Marie Segal—look for them chickens!"

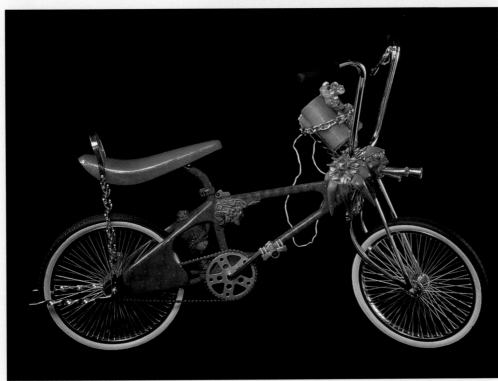

Well, that about does it for your tour of my favorite clay projects and techniques. I hope you have had fun, fun, fun and learned a lot about polymer clay.

Now, if you don't mind, I'm off to watch the sunset, eat smoked oysters, and drink bourbon and Diet Coke with my friends. I'll clean that messy clay table tomorrow.

Metric equivalency chart

mm–millimetres   cm–centimetres
inches to millimetres and centimetres

inches	mm	cm	inches	cm	inches	cm	inches	cm
⅛	3	0.3	6	15.2	21	53.3	36	91.4
¼	6	0.6	7	17.8	22	55.9	37	94.0
⅜	10	1.0	8	20.3	23	58.4	38	96.5
½	13	1.3	9	22.9	24	61.0	39	99.1
⅝	16	1.6	10	25.4	25	63.5	40	101.6
¾	19	1.9	11	27.9	26	66.0	41	104.1
⅞	22	2.2	12	30.5	27	68.6	42	106.7
1	25	2.5	13	33.0	28	71.1	43	109.2
1¼	32	3.2	14	35.6	29	73.7	44	111.8
1½	38	3.8	15	38.1	30	76.2	45	114.3
1¾	44	4.4	16	40.6	31	78.7	46	116.8
2	51	5.1	17	43.2	32	81.3	47	119.4
3	76	7.6	18	45.7	33	83.8	48	121.9
4	102	10.2	19	48.3	34	86.4	49	124.5
5	127	12.7	20	50.8	35	88.9	50	127.0

Index

3-D Chain-linked Necklace — 55
Additional Tools — 13
Allowing the Clay to Rest — 23
Antiquing Polymer Clay — 25
Backpack Clip — 63
Baking the Clay — 19
Baking Tips — 20
Barrette — 67
Basic Clay Tools — 12
Bracelet — 94
Brooch — 96
Buttons — 42
Cernit — 16
Choosing Clay — 14
Clay Frame — 38
Clay Is Too Hard — 19
Clay Is Too Soft — 19
Clay Just Keeps Crumbling — 19
Clay Turns Dark In the Oven — 19
Conditioning the Clay — 16
Conditioning the Clay by Hand — 16
Conditioning the Clay Using a Clay-dedicated Food Processor — 17
Conditioning the Clay Using a Clay-dedicated Pasta Machine — 17
Covered Pen — 48
Earrings — 30
FIMO — 14
Finishing Polymer Clay — 25
Flower Drawer Pulls — 60
For the Sake of Reference — 18
Fossils Light Switch Cover — 86
Getting Started — 12
Goddess Polymeria, The by Z Kripke — 9
Heart Earrings — 80
How do I add a banner to the bull's eye cane? — 42
How do I make 3-D chain-linked canes? — 55
How do I make a blended cane using the Skinner method? — 51

How do I make a bull's eye cane? — 38
How do I make a checkerboard cane? — 48
How do I make a face cane? — 67
How do I make a feather cane? — 46
How do I make a heart-shaped cane? — 80
How do I make a millefiori bead? — 63
How do I make a mold? — 88
How do I make a Natasha bead? — 100
How do I make a pinroll cane? — 28
How do I make a shaman cane? — 75
How do I make a simple flower cane? — 60
How do I make a snowman cane? — 72
How do I make a star cane? — 64
How do I make clay look metallic? — 96
How do I recombine the pinroll cane? — 32
How do I resize and reshape a pinroll cane? — 30
How do I turn the pinroll cane inside out? — 34
How do I use clay molds? — 84
How do I use colored pencils with clay? — 92
How do I use household objects to make a reverse impression? — 86
How do I use rubber stamps with clay? — 94
How do I use scrap clay? — 98
How do I use the banner cane? — 44
How do I use the bull's eye cane? — 40
How to Use This Book — 8
Introduction — 8
Lacy Ornament — 40
Lapel Pin — 64
Leaf Light Switch Cover — 84
Light Switch Cover — 51
Liquid Sculpey — 15
Making Basic Canes — 21
Mobius Bead — 34
Mold Release — 23
Napkin Rings — 32
Natasha Bead — 100
Need Green Clay But Don't Have Any — 19

Polymer Clay for the First Time — 8
Postage Stamp Collage — 46
Postcard — 75
Rainbow Coasters — 92
Reducing & Reshaping a Cane — 21
Rolling Sheets of Clay — 17
Rolling the Clay Out by Hand — 17
Rolling the Clay Using a Pasta Machine — 17
Safely Using Polymer Clay — 16
Sanding Polymer Clay — 25
Sculpey — 14
Sculpey III — 14
Sculpey Granitex — 15
Sculpey Premo — 15
Sculpey Super Flex — 15
Sealants for Polymer Clay — 25
Seashell Box — 88
Section 1: Polymer Clay Basics — 10
Section 2: Basic Canes — 26
Section 3: Pictorial Canes — 58
Section 4: Molds & Textural Effects — 82
Section 5: Gallery — 102
Simple Molds — 23
Small Candleholder — 28
Snowman Pin — 72
Super Sculpey — 14
To Reduce a Round Cane — 21
To Reshape and Reduce a Square Cane — 22
To Reshape and Reduce a Triangular Cane — 22
To Reshape and Reduce an Oval Cane — 23
Tools — 12
Troubleshooting with Clay — 19
Twisted Beads — 44
Using Molds — 23
Using Rubber Stamps with Polymer Clay — 24
Using Translucent Heat-embossing Powders with Polymer Clay — 24
Valentine's Day Pin — 98
What do I need to get started? — 12